THE
DUKE & DUCHESS
OF CAMBRIDGE

THE
DUKE & DUCHESS
OF CAMBRIDGE

AN ILLUSTRATED COMPANION
CELEBRATING THE BIRTH OF
HRH PRINCE GEORGE OF CAMBRIDGE
22 JULY 2013

JAMES MALONEY

CONSTABLE • LONDON

The publishers would like to thank William Gardiner, Mo McFarland and Paulo Silva for their help in accessing photographs from the *Daily Mail* archives.

Constable & Robinson Ltd
55-56 Russell Square
London WC1B 4HP

First published in the UK in 2013 by Constable,
an imprint of Constable & Robinson Ltd,
in association with The *Daily Mail*

A copy of the British Library Cataloguing in Publication Data is available from the British Library

ISBN 978-1-4721-0963-7

Designed by Design 23, London

Printed and bound in Great Britain by Butler Tanner & Dennis Ltd, Frome, Somerset

All photographs supplied from the Daily Mail Photo Archive except for the following: page 20 bottom Rex Features; page 23 top left and right Rex Features; page 24 bottom left Rex Features; page 35 Rex Features; page 40 Stephen Lock/Rex Features; page 43 Rex Features; page 44 Rex Features; page 55 top and bottom Brendan Beirne/Rex Features; page 58 top left Rex Features, top right James Fraser/Rex Features; pages 70 and 71 Rex Features; page 75 Rex Features; pages 78 and 79 Axelle/Bauer-Griffin. com; page 95 Dominic O'Neill/Rex features; page 96 Dominic O'Neill Rex Features; page 106 Rex Features; page 121 top AP Photo/Peter Morrison; pages 148 and 149 UPI/Heinz Ruckemann/Eyevine; page 150 top left Rex Features; page 153 John Nguyen/JN Visuals; page 162 Paul Grover/Rex Features; page 169 top AP Photo/Mark Baker; page 170 bottom right Tim Rooke/Rex Features; page 171 and 172 Rex Features; page 185-190,192 Press Association

CONTENTS

It's every young girl's dream to meet and marry a handsome Prince and in some respects there is a fairy tale quality to Kate Middleton's life.

She may have not been exactly a rags-to-riches Cinderella – on the contrary, she was the eldest daughter of prosperous parents – but she was certainly not from an aristocratic background, which is the usual circle in which British Royals meet their future spouses. Her parents were firmly middle-class made good. And going back just a little further into the past the link is solid working-class.

When Catherine's mother, Carole, was born, her first home was a council flat in West London. She comes from a long line of coal miners, her forebears having worked long hours underground in awful conditions, scraping by on very little money to keep their heads above the poverty line.

Over successive generations the family's lot gradually improved. Carole, an airline stewardess, met and married work colleague Michael, who became a flight despatcher, and they bought a nice home near Reading, Berkshire. But it was Carole's idea to supply children's partyware that evolved into the incredibly successful online business that made them millionaires.

It enabled them to send their daughter to prestigious fee paying schools that led to St Andrews University where she was to form a friendship with a shy fellow 'fresher', Prince William.

Their friendship developed into a student romance away from the glare of publicity. It was allowed the time to build into a strong relationship as they gradually came to know each other. Like most relationships, there were some hiccups along the way but the setbacks made them stronger and wiser. Even spending time apart only led to them realising that what they both actually wanted was to be together.

He took a long time to propose, though, and carefully chose what he considered to be the right time and the right place. Their picture-book wedding, which took place at the historic Westminster Abbey, was in the best grand tradition of royal weddings but with a 'natural' and 'environmental' twist that was all Catherine's.

With church bells ringing and crowds cheering, they made their way through the streets of London back to Buckingham Palace as husband and wife, where they displayed their love, as the waiting throng demanded, with a kiss on the palace balcony. In fact, they enjoyed it so much that they kissed again!

The crowd loved it but then Kate has always known how to please a crowd and to make people feel happy and at ease. She's the 'commoner' with the common touch. Wherever she goes, she engages with members of the public in a natural and unaffected way with her ready smile, infectious giggle and upbeat nature.

She doesn't put on 'airs and graces'. She's simply herself and can mix with people from all social backgrounds. That's what is so special about her.

She has barely put a foot wrong in the public eye – from royal girlfriend, through to fiancée and finally, bride. Public engagements and royal duties are carried out with charm and aplomb, yet it all seems unforced and remarkably natural. She is never over-awed and has always remained confident and at ease. These are the qualities that will serve her well.

Kate, or Catherine, as William took to calling her in the days leading up to their marriage is now officially Her Royal Highness Princess William, Duchess of Cambridge, Countess of Strathearn, Baroness Carrickfergus. Yet she has sensibly never lost sight of her comparatively ordinary background. The public still think that she is 'one of us' who happened to meet a prince and marry into royalty.

Now in line to become a future Queen of England, Kate has never lost sight of her roots. This book, liberally illustrated with glorious and rare photographs, charts her remarkable story from middle-class childhood to royal bride. And, as the pictures and words will tell, although her life has changed to an almost unimaginable degree, her essence and personality have remained the same throughout.

Prince William was only too aware of the strained marriage between his mother, the late Princess Diana, and his father, Prince Charles. This made him cautious in choosing the right woman to be his bride. That he loved Kate never really seems to have been in doubt, yet he knew he had to be careful about exposing her to the pressures of life as a 'Royal'. Both he and Kate had to be sure that she was ready to cope with the stress of becoming one of the most photographed women on the planet.

He may have taken his time, but it seems that he chose very well. Both the public and the Royal Family have taken her to their hearts and William and Kate's body language and eye contact when they are together shows that they are very much in love – as is evident in many of the photographs within these pages.

Sometimes, you see, fairy tales really do come true!

PREVIOUS SPREAD: Catherine wears a head-dress of fresh flowers in the Solomon Islands, September 2012.

RIGHT: Catherine backlit by glorious southern hemisphere sunshine when she and Prince William toured Southeast Asia and the Pacific, September 2012.

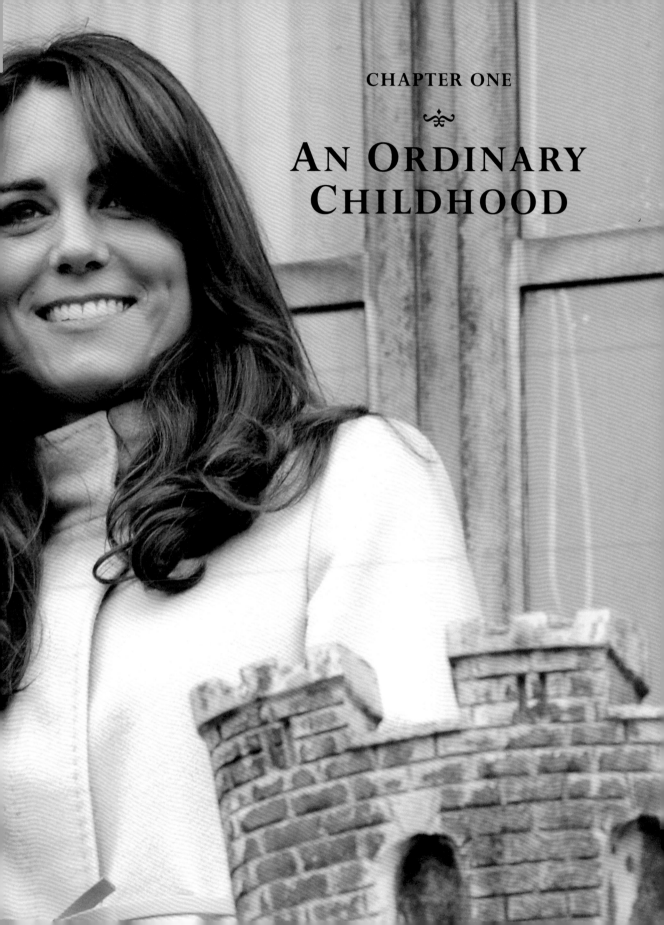

CHAPTER ONE

AN ORDINARY CHILDHOOD

There was nothing out of the ordinary about Catherine Middleton's early life. In fact, it was the very essence of middle-class, middle-England ordinariness. And delving back just two generations earlier – on her mother's side of the family – her roots were very much what would be described as 'working class'.

The long road to the grandeur of Buckingham Palace and her place as future Queen is the kind of rags-to-riches fairy-tale that young girls dream of. For Catherine – better known as Kate and, more officially, The Duchess of Cambridge – comes from a long line of coal miners, carpenters and general labourers, including a humble street sweeper. The paternal side of her family was more affluent and included cloth merchants, bankers and solicitors, but there was also a relative who was locked up in one of Her Majesty's prisons!

Kate Middleton's maternal ancestors, the Harrisons, lived and worked in the grimy and dingy streets of the mining communities in the North East of England. Her great-great-great-great grandfather, James Harrison, was born in 1796 in Byker, Tyne and Wear and lived with his wife Jane and their children in one of the area's many run-down terraced houses. He worked as a miner in the Byker Colliery. Later, they moved to Low Moorsley, a small village just outside Hetton-le-Hole, where a new mine had been sunk.

Toiling in the mines was laborious and dangerous. It was also very poorly paid considering the physical hardship endured by those working in the pits. Miners would spend hours deep beneath the ground without seeing natural light until it was time to go home at the end of the day. Their food was passed down to them and coal dust got everywhere, eventually becoming so engrained in the skin that no amount of scrubbing could properly get rid of it.

James was followed down the pit by two of his six children – John and Septimus. John married miner's daughter Jane Liddell and they shared a small, 'two-up, two-down' terraced house with their 10 children. One of them was Kate's great-great-grandfather, John, who was born in 1874 and tragically orphaned, along with his siblings, at the age of 14, when their parents died from tuberculosis, at that time commonly called 'consumption'. Two years later, John began working down the mine and was later killed whilst fighting in the final months of the First World War in 1918.

The social climb out of the mine began with John's son, Thomas – Kate's great grandfather. Born in 1904, he was apprenticed to his maternal grandfather as a carpenter. After serving in the Second World War, he and

PREVIOUS SPREAD: The Duchess of Cambridge waves to crowds from the balcony of the Guildhall in Cambridge, November 2012.

LEFT: An early royal connection as Prince Philip returns from a trip to South America to be greeted by the manager of Heathrow, with pilot Peter Middleton, Catherine's grandfather, in the background, October 1966.

his wife, Elizabeth, moved to Sunderland for a while before making the long journey south to settle in Southall, West London. They had two daughters – Ruth was the first, followed by Dorothy, who was to become Kate Middleton's grandmother.

Born in 1935, Dorothy was ambitious to improve her lot in life. Her 'airs and graces' earned her the nickname of 'Lady Dorothy' amongst some members of her family. She worked as a shop assistant before marrying Ronald Goldsmith in 1953. Prior to being called up to do his National Service, Ronald had dabbled in a variety of jobs and on his return he worked as a haulage driver and then as an engineer for his brother-in-law. He later set up his own business as a builder.

Ronald and Dorothy managed to earn enough money to be able to move out of their council house and buy their own home.

Dorothy's daughter, Carole, born in 1955, shared her mother's aspirations. The family moved to a semi-detached house in Norwood, South London, when Carole was 11, a year after her brother, Gary, was born. On leaving school she worked as an airline stewardess where she met handsome trainee pilot, Michael Middleton.

The Middletons hailed from Leeds, West Yorkshire and, far removed from the squalor of the mines, they had a family history as solicitors.

Kate's great-great-great grandfather, William Middleton, born in 1807, was the son of a joiner and cabinetmaker from Wakefield. William was the first in the family to become a solicitor and, whilst working in Leeds, he met and married Mary Ward, the daughter of a milliner, with whom he had eight children. After she died at the age of 48, he married his sister-in-law, Sarah Ward and moved to a mansion in Chapel Allerton where they employed two servants.

His son, John, also became a solicitor, as did his son, Noel – Kate's great-grandfather. Noel, who fought in the First World War, married Olive Lupton in 1914. She was from a well-to-do family in Leeds who had made their fortune as wool merchants in the 18th century. Olive was educated at the prestigious girl's private school, Roedean, in Sussex.

Olive's paternal grandmother, Fanny, was descended from Sir Thomas Fairfax, a Parliamentarian general in the English Civil War who moulded the New Model Army which inflicted a historic defeat on the Royalists at the battle of Naseby in 1645.

By coincidence, Prince William is also descended from Fairfax through the Spencer line, making Kate and William fifteenth cousins.

Noel and Olive's third son, Peter, Kate's grandfather, was born in 1920 and joined the RAF, serving in WWII. His love of flying stayed

RIGHT: Catherine as an expectant mother with William at Westminster Abbey for the Queen's Coronation 60th Anniversary service, June 2013.

with him after the end of the war and he became a civilian pilot. Later
he married Valerie Glassborow, the daughter of a bank manager named
Frederick. When Peter got a job as a pilot instructor at Heathrow
Airport, he moved his family to Beaconsfield in Buckinghamshire.

The Glassborows had been bank messengers and clerks before
Frederick had made the leap to bank manager. But the ancestral line had
not been completely respectable as it is recorded that, in 1881, Kate's
great-great-great grandfather, Edward Thomas Glassborow (Frederick's
father), a messenger, served time behind bars in Holloway Prison, in
North London.

Peter and Valerie Middleton's second son, Michael, born in Leeds in
1949, had his head in the skies, like his father, and trained to be a pilot
but later switched to ground crew. It was while working at Heathrow in
the mid-70s that he met air hostess Carole Goldsmith and they moved in
together in a flat in Slough, Berkshire.

In 1979 he was promoted to flight dispatcher for BA at Heathrow,
an important role with responsibility for checking that everything is in
order and ready to go on a plane before it takes off.

Michael and Carole married on 21 June 1980, at St James the
Less church in Dorney, Buckinghamshire, which dates back to the 12th
century. The couple bought a modest red brick, late Victorian, four-
bedroom semi in the rural village of Bradfield Southend, near Reading,
Berkshire. The village has a community-owned shop and post office, a
doctor's surgery, garden centre, garage and at the end of the road where
the Middletons lived was a picturesque pub named the Queen's Head.

Catherine (known as Kate) was the couple's first child and was born
on 9 January 1982 at the Royal Berkshire Hospital in Reading. She was
Christened at St Andrew's Bradfield, Berkshire, a large and imposing
grey-stoned church, on 20 June of that year. Michael wore a dark suit
and diagonally-striped tie and Carole a floral dress from Laura Ashley.

As a young girl, Kate's bedroom was what one might describe as
'snug', being one of two rooms with sloping ceilings situated under the
eaves. But after the arrival of her sister, Pippa, on 6 September 1983,
and later her brother James, she moved to a large bedroom downstairs
on the first floor.

Carole took Kate to a mothers-and-toddlers playgroup held in the
hall of another local church, St Peter's. But when Kate was two, there
was a big upheaval as the family moved to Amman in Jordan, where
Michael had a temporary posting with British Airways. Carole, at this
time, was on extended maternity leave with eight-month-old Pippa.

They lived in a two-storey rented villa close to a park and at the age of three Kate was enrolled at the local nursery which had a mixture of children, aged between three and five, including Jordanians, British, Indonesian and American, who were taught in both Arabic and English.

There were close to one hundred children in total who were split into small classes. Kate was in a class of twelve. The day started at 8.00 a.m. with the youngsters sitting in a circle where they would give a rousing rendition of Incy Wincy Spider, both in English and Arabic. This was followed by a short verse from the Quran in order both to improve the children's Arabic and to teach them about such concepts as respect and love.

At 9.30 a.m. they would have breakfast of hummus, cheese and labneh – a Middle Eastern dish in which Greek yogurt is strained and rolled into light, spreadable cheese.

The children enjoyed caring for and feeding the rabbits and ducks and also had fun in the sandpit. Every now and then they would put on plays for the parents to watch.

Christmas was celebrated, with the nursery's founder, Mrs Nabulsi, dressing as Santa Claus and Ramadan was also observed.

Twice a month there would be visits to nearby places of interest. A particular favourite was the Haya Cultural Centre, with its playgrounds, library, museum and arts and crafts rooms.

The nursery day ended at 12.30 p.m. when Kate was usually collected by her mother. But occasionally her father would arrive, looking smart in his British Airways uniform, which caused a stir of excitement amongst the young children.

The Middletons returned home to Berkshire in September 1986, after Michael's posting came to an end. It was timed so that Kate could go to school shortly afterwards. She attended a pre-school nursery at St Peter's church hall for a while and it was around this time that Carole started a venture that would evolve into a highly successful business that was to make the family fortune.

Frustrated at not being able to find any decent party paraphernalia for her children's birthday celebrations, or value-for-money 'goodie-bags' for her children's friends to take home with them, she started to make her own. They proved to be so popular with her friends that she began making and selling them to other parents for their own children's parties.

Kate briefly attended the local school, Bradfield Church of England Primary, at the end of their road, where she discovered an early flair for

RIGHT: Catherine excelled at sports at St Andrew's School in Pangbourne, Berkshire. She is in the middle of the back row in the netball team photo and third from the left in the swimming photo.

TOP: Catherine in the
middle of the front row of
the rounders team …

BOTTOM: … and third
from left in tennis.

sporting activities such as rounders and swimming. Later she was enrolled
at a private school, St. Andrew's, in Pangbourne, where she remained until
July 1995. Kate thoroughly enjoyed her time here, where her love for sport
flourished, and she told her mother that one day she wanted to return there
as a member of staff.

The school kept guinea pigs and Kate and her sister Pippa liked
them so much that they were allowed to name one each. Pippa's was
named Pip and Catherine's Squeak.

Catherine took up the recorder and then the flute which she
played in the school orchestra. Her natural ability for sport led to her
captaining the hockey team and she was leading goal scorer in 1995. She
also distinguished herself in the high jump and in the 4x100 relay team.

Recalling her time at the school, Deputy Head teacher Richard
Hudson told the BBC, 'She held our record for the high jump … for
about 20 years she's had that. She was very hard working, very polite
and friendly and very kind to the younger children.'

Kate also found confidence in front of other people by taking part
in public speaking competitions and drama groups. In a school play, a
video of which surfaced in 2011, she takes centre stage, aged 12, as a
pretty peasant girl in a white shift with white flowers in her hair. Whilst
out walking she meets a fortune teller who tells her that she will meet
a handsome and rich man who will fall in love with her and marry her.
Later, she meets the man. His name? William. Maybe that 'fortune
teller' should have turned professional!

Meanwhile, back at home, Michael and Carole's third child, James
William, was born on 15 April 1987 and this was the year that Carole
turned her party bags hobby into a serious business by launching Party
Pieces, a mail order catalogue company run from the large shed at the
bottom of their garden.

At the age of age of eight, Kate and Pippa joined the local Brownies
group at St Peter's Church hall. The girls particularly enjoyed summer
camping expeditions to woods as well as visits to farms to see the animals
and understand what it was like to work on a farm.

Meanwhile, Party Pieces blossomed into a huge success and Carole
took the opportunity to capitalise with the rapid growth and influence of
the internet by putting Party Pieces online. It was the perfect vehicle for
the business, enabling it to reach all corners of the UK. As the business
flourished, the Middletons moved to a more substantial five-bedroom
house in July 1995 in nearby Chapel Row in Bucklebury – a picture-
book English village, with a green, a pub and a butcher's.

That September Kate moved to fee-paying Downe House School, an all-girls boarding establishment just outside Newbury, Berkshire. But after two terms here she left to go to the prestigious Marlborough College in Wiltshire, which takes in both girls and boys.

Kate was very happy at Malborough and did well in class and on the sports field. She gained 11 GCSEs and three A Levels in Art, Biology and Chemistry and represented her school at tennis, hockey, netball and athletics where she excelled at high jump. She also gained her Duke of Edinburgh's Gold Award, which involved a four day hike. Fellow pupils recalled her as being fun, polite, kind and sporty.

Nicholas Sampson, master at the college, said that she was a 'bright, popular and extremely capable pupil.'

Kate was to spend four years at Marlborough, leaving in July 2000, and then took a traditional gap year. Her love of art took her to Italy that September where she enrolled on a twelve-week course at the British Institute in Florence.

Founded in 1917 to promote cultural exchange between Italy and the English-speaking world, the Institute offers Italian and English language courses alongside the History of Italian Art from the Medieval and Renaissance period.

The Institute has two locations. The language department is at the Palazzo Strozzino, which was built in 1458, and the art courses are at the grand Palazzo Lanfredini on the south bank of the River Arno. This was formerly owned by Evelyn Waugh's writer friend, Sir Harold Acton, who bequeathed it to the Institute when he died in 1994.

Prince Charles and Princess Diana visited the Institute in 1985, when Charles became one of its two patrons.

Here, Kate spent three hours a day from Monday to Friday learning the Italian language and all about the Renaissance while staying in student digs, arranged by the Institute, above a delicatessen. She enjoyed tours to Florence's wonderful art museums, churches, duomos and palaces with their overwhelming display of masterpieces by the likes of Michelangelo, da Vinci and Botticelli. There were also cultural trips to nearby Sienna and San Gimignano.

When she wasn't studying, Kate could be found relaxing over a cocktail in the L'Art Bar. Here, the reasonably priced but well prepared and presented cocktails proved extremely popular with students. The strawberry dacquari was a particular favourite of hers.

After this glorious immersion into the heady beauty and richness of Renaissance art, she followed in Prince William's footsteps by joining a

TOP LEFT: Catherine talks to a class at her old school, St Andrew's, recalling that she once said she'd like to return as a teacher, November 2012.

TOP RIGHT: Trying out the new artificial sports pitch at St Andrew's, November, 2012.

BOTTOM: Catherine, closest to the birthday girl, at Angharad Allford's first birthday party.

TOP AND BOTTOM RIGHT:
Messing around with
friends at Marlborough in
2000.

BOTTOM LEFT:
Catherine, third from
left, in Patagonia, Chile
on an Operation Raleigh
expedition in January
2001.

group of volunteers for a ten-week Raleigh International expedition to
Patagonia in Chile in January 2001.

The Prince had gone to Chile with Raleigh International a year
earlier where he helped to build an adventure playground in the village
of Tortel.

In her first three weeks in the country Kate, along with her fellow
volunteers, trekked through the wilderness carrying her food and kit in
a rucksack. This was followed by a three-week stint helping scientists
study marine life when she spent a lot of time in an inflatable boat,
collecting samples. The remainder of the course saw her complete the
construction of a new fire station, with Kate helping to fit its windows
and roof cladding.

Former expedition leader, Malcolm Sotherland, recalled that Kate
was 'a hard worker and got on well with everyone. She embraced
everything that was thrown at her. She was a very mature girl for
her age. She knew what she was about. She knew how to look after
herself.'

Her busy and adventurous gap year included joining the crew of a
Round the World Challenge yacht in the Solent. Kate sailed every day
and her duties included keeping the boat clean and serving food and
drink to guests.

Soon she would be going to university and the choice she made would
bring her into contact with a fellow student who would ultimately change
her life in ways that she could never have imagined.

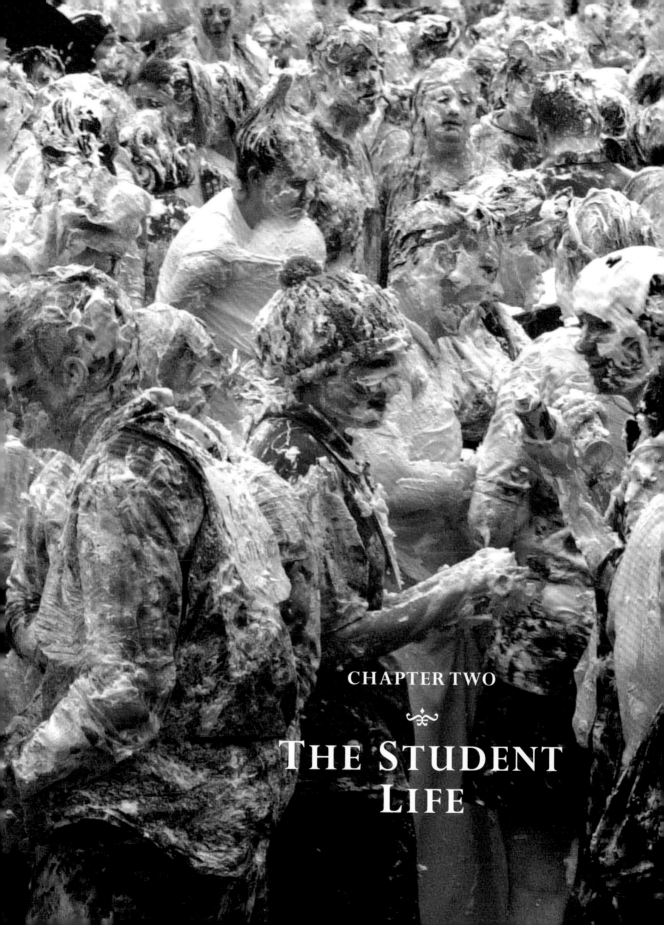

CHAPTER TWO

❧

THE STUDENT
LIFE

The city of St Andrews, situated by the sea in Fife, Scotland, has an ancient and colourful history dating back to the medieval age.

The earliest inhabitants were farmers and fishermen, but pilgrims and monks arrived in great numbers from across Europe after the legend grew that the bones of the Christian apostle St Andrew had been brought there.

St Andrew was adopted as the patron saint of Scotland and Celtic monks built a chapel for worship near the harbour. As its association with religion grew, a great Cathedral was constructed in St Andrews in 1160, bringing great prestige to the city.

Medieval St Andrews had two friaries, one founded by the Dominicans (Blackfriars), and later another by the Franciscans (Greyfriars). The imposing St Andrews Castle was built around the year 1200 and had a dual use as both fortress and residential palace for the Bishops and Archbishops of the city.

In 1413 a university was established which is still going strong today – the very first university in Scotland and the third oldest in the English-speaking world.

The Calvinist John Knox, a leader of the Protestant Reformation, studied at the university. He was ordained to the Catholic priesthood in 1536 but joined the movement to reform the Scottish church, leading to bloodshed in 1546 with the murder of Cardinal Beaton, the Archbishop of St Andrews and leader of the anti-Protestant movement who had orchestrated the trial and executions of 'heretics'.

Whilst preaching in the city Knox was taken prisoner by French Catholic forces and exiled to England. On his return to St Andrews in 1559 he led the Protestant Reformation in partnership with Scottish Protestant nobles.

Today, the sites where various Protestant martyrs met their deaths are commemorated throughout St Andrews. For students at the university, the most notable are the letters PH, marked out with cobblestones outside the main gate of St Salvator's College. They refer to Patrick Hamilton, a member of the university who became Scotland's first protestant martyr at the age of just 24 when Cardinal Beaton ordered him to be burned at the stake for heresy on that very spot.

According to student tradition, if anyone treads on the initials they will be cursed and will fail their degree. So they are stepped or jumped over. Should anyone set foot on them, the only way to prevent the curse from taking place is to participate in the annual

PREVIOUS SPREAD:
The traditional, 'Raisin Weekend' foam fight at St Andrews University.

LEFT: Catherine enjoying some summer sun during the Olympics in London, July 2012.

May Dip. Held at dawn on May Day, students get into the spirit of things by warming themselves with alcohol at various inns around the city and then at dawn they gather, wearing their red gowns, to make their way down to the beach in a candle-lit procession.

Many enjoy a barbecue by a beach bonfire before taking the plunge, casting off their outer clothes and charging into the bitter cold North Sea in their swimwear, although some brave souls dare to bare!

If all this history were not enough, St Andrews is also regarded as the birthplace of golf. The first documented mention of golf in Scotland appears in a 1457 Act of the Scottish Parliament, in which King James II of Scotland prohibits the playing of the games of 'gowf' and football as these were a distraction from archery practice for military purposes.

In 1552, a charter, bearing the seal of the Archbishop of St Andrews, confirms that townspeople had the right to play golf on the Links, which at that time were also used for activities such as football, livestock grazing and rabbit breeding

Over the centuries, the popularity of golf grew and in 1754 22 'noblemen and gentlemen of the Kingdom of Fife' formed themselves into the Society of St Andrews Golfers. Eighty years later, this Society was to evolve into the Royal and Ancient Golf Club of St Andrews. By this point the society had already established such precedents as ruling that a round of golf should be 18 holes in length. The R&A published the first 'Rules of Golf' in 1897 and since then it has been recognised as the sport's ruling body throughout the world.

Into this richly historic city came Kate Middleton in 2001, taking care to step over the PH cobbles outside St Salvator's gate as she took her place as a student at the university to study History of Art.

She took up residence at St Salvator's Hall, situated on the quadrangle in the heart of the university buildings. Affectionately known by students as 'Sallies', the Hall, a rambling stone brick building, is regarded as one of the most prestigious residences. It accommodates 190 students over three floors in furnished bedrooms with shared kitchen and bathroom facilities.

'Sallies' has a long-standing tradition of 'High Table' which sees a small group of selected students attending a formal dinner in the dining room when they dress formally in their undergraduate gowns to join a prominent member of the community and/or academic

staff for dinner. Everyone gets a chance to sit at High Table and it is regarded by students as one of the highlights of their year.

The oak-panelled dining hall with its stained glass windows commemorating founders and benefactors of the university is the most impressive room in the building. The spacious Common Room has a grand piano, a television and daily newspapers. There is also a library and a computer/study room.

In the basement there is a snooker table, a table-tennis table, laundry room and a projector which can be used for films or games.

A team of wardens lives in the residence, there to help students with advice and general pastoral care. In addition there are various porters, kitchen and cleaning staff and service managers.

Kate's room had a desk, wardrobe, bookcase and wash basin. Along the corridor was a bathroom.

Freshers' Week is organised to integrate new students into life at the university, introducing traditions, arranging parties and games and hosting the official ball. First year students, or 'freshers', are adopted by older students who act as their Academic 'parents', providing support and advice. Kate, like most other freshers, eagerly participated but one newcomer had delayed his arrival because he specifically wanted to avoid this active first week.

Mindful of the overwhelming press attention that his mother, Princess Diana, received during her life, 19-year-old Prince William decided that St Andrews University, set in a remote, wind-swept corner of the British Isles, was the ideal place for him to study.

Like Kate, he had enjoyed a gap year which included a ten-week Raleigh expedition to Chile, followed by three-and-a-half months in Africa learning about the wildlife and environment. Now he was ready to knuckle down and concentrate on his degree subject – History of Art.

Before he arrived, William spoke at a press conference about why he chose this particular university and how he hoped to settle in.

'I want to go there and be an ordinary student. I mean, I'm only going to university. It's not like I'm getting married, though that's what it feels like sometimes,' he said, feeling a little uncomfortable at the attention. He hoped that he would soon be able to blend in as a normal student.

'It will get easier as time goes on. Everyone will get bored of me – which they do,' he said. 'But people who try to take advantage of me and get a piece of me, I spot it quickly and soon go off them.

'The reason I didn't want to go to an English university is because I have lived there and wanted to get away and try somewhere else. I also knew I would be seeing a lot of Wales in the future. And I do love Scotland. There is plenty of space, I love the hills and mountains and I thought St Andrews had a real community feel to it.'

Although he was studying History of Art, the Prince thought his future interest in life would be in another direction, one that he had experienced during his gap year. 'I'm much more interested in doing something with the environment, but I'm not sure what yet,' he said.

There was a buzz around the university that year because, of course, all the other students knew he was coming. After it was first publicly announced that the Prince would be enrolling at St Andrews, there was a huge demand for places there. Applications increased by 44 per cent.

William later explained that his late arrival was due to him wanting to keep as low a profile as possible.

'It would have been a media frenzy and that's not fair on the other new students,' he said before adding in jocular fashion, 'Plus, I thought I would probably end up in a gutter completely wrecked, and the people I had met that week wouldn't end up being my friends anyway. It also meant I could have another week's holiday.'

But William insisted that he wanted to make friends with students from all backgrounds.

'It's not as if I choose my friends on the basis of where they are from or what they are,' he said. 'It's about their character and who they are and whether we get on. I just hope I can meet people I get on with. I don't care about their backgrounds.'

William was driven down from Balmoral with his father, Prince Charles, arriving at the university shortly before 5.00 p.m. on Sunday 23 September 2001. A crowd of around 2,000 watched the car drive into the quadrangle where William emerged, dressed in casual student attire of blue sweater, jeans and trainers, along with his father, to be met by university principal Dr Brian Lang before a brief walk along the road to greet the crowds. After a few minutes, William entered his hall of residence – St Salvator's.

Kate threw herself into the social side of university life and she beamed from ear to ear as she took part in the traditional Raisin Weekend in the second week of November.

RIGHT: Prince William at St Andrews University posing for the press in return for being left in peace.

LEFT: Prince William has eyes only for the catwalk during the now famous student fashion show where Catherine was one of the models.

The origin of this, St Andrews' most bizarre and riotous ritual, is that older students would traditionally introduce new students to the town and receive by way of thanks a pound of raisins. But it has developed over the years into madcap mayhem!

The modern version sees each 'child' fresher report to their 'mother's' house for 'afternoon tea' on a Sunday, which starts early, around 11.00 a.m. 'Tea' often, but not always, involves alcohol with the food. This is followed by 'family games' which range from drinking games to scavenger hunts.

In the evening the 'fathers' often take their 'children' on pub crawls. The following morning, each 'child' visits their 'father's' house to present a traditional gift of a pound of raisins (a modern twist swaps this for a bottle of wine), in exchange for a 'raisin receipt.' This can be a traditional one with an appropriate Latin phrase but has increasingly been anything from old washing machines to sofas! As long as it has a Latin phrase written on it, it will pass for a receipt.

The child then leaves with the receipt and visits his or her mother, where he/she is fancy-dressed in whatever outfit is deemed appropriate.

All the first year 'children' then head for the Quad to drop off the receipts in a skip before the climax of the ritual – a mass shaving-foam fight.

Kate joined the other freshers, dressing as a little girl with her hair tied in two bunches and bright red painted cheeks. But William, mindful of his royal responsibilities and only too aware of how much attention he attracted, even amongst the students, withdrew from such frivolities. He also refrained from joining sports teams or the many university societies. It resulted in him feeling rather lonely and sad in his first year, in which he missed his family and friends.

But he regularly came into contact with lively Kate. The pair were studying the same course and he would also bump into her on his way to and from his room. He was intrigued and wanted to get to know her better but also cautious and a little shy.

Kate started dating Rupert Finch, a 22-year-old law student in his final year. Meanwhile, William started quietly dating Carley Massy-Birch, a second year English language and creative-writing student. Their romance remained under the radar and attracted little attention from the outside world. She was later to describe it as 'a university thing.'

Come the weekends and William couldn't wait to get back to Highgrove, his father's home in Gloucestershire. Whenever he was home, he took the opportunity to see Arabella Musgrave, a girl he had known since childhood. She was the 18-year-old daughter of Major Nicholas Musgrave, who managed the Cirencester Park Polo Club, where Prince Charles played. Their long friendship had taken a romantic turn just months before he went to St Andrews in the summer of 2001.

But gradually Kate and William became closer and formed a friendship. William felt that she was someone whom he could trust and confide in and that December he admitted to her that he was so unhappy that he was thinking of dropping out of university. Kate encouraged him to stay and said that specialising in Geography instead of History of Art might suit him better. She also tactfully suggested that he spent more weekends in St Andrews to get used to the people and the place instead of returning to Highgrove at every opportunity. During William's Christmas holiday, his father also urged him to stay on and he duly returned to St Andrews, switching to studying Geography. From then on, he began to enjoyed university far more.

In March, Kate took part in the annual student union charity fashion show where her startling outfit left William – who had paid £200 for a front-row ticket – wide-eyed as she sashayed down the cat-walk in a see-through black lace dress over a black bandeau bra and briefs. At the after-show party, William made a beeline for Kate and they chatted together for most of the rest of the evening.

That July Kate earned some money serving drinks at Henley Regatta for a catering firm called Snatch Bar, owned by 22-year-old Robert Laing, whom she knew from Marlborough. Laing, whose great aunt was Princess Diana's grandmother, Lady Ruth Fermoy, commented, 'I only pay Kate £5 an hour, but she's a pretty girl so she should get lots of tips.'

Back at St Andrews, an inner circle of friends was gradually forming involving Kate, William, Ginny Fraser, whose father Lord Strathalmond was a Lloyd's underwriter, colonel's daughter Olivia Bleasdale who was also studying History of Art, and William's friend from Eton, Fergus Boyd.

Kate and Fergus persuaded William to join the university water polo team and it really helped him to come out of his shell.

Later, Kate, William, Fergus and Olivia moved out of 'Sallies' and into a four-bedroom Victorian two-storey terraced town house

LEFT: Designer Charlotte Todd shows off the dress she created …

RIGHT: … and Catherine models it on the catwalk, March 2002.

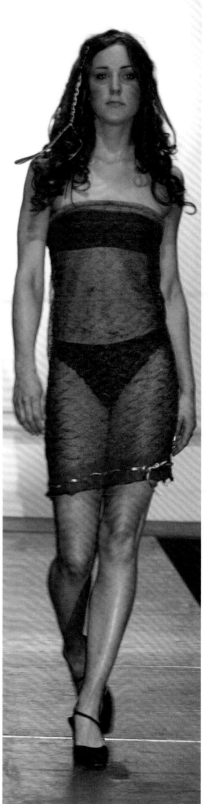

LEFT: Catherine in model mode once again, this time at the Game Fair at Blenheim Palace, August 2004.

at 13a Hope Street. The sandstone house is one of many similar residences on the prestigious street, lit outside by Victorian-style street lamps. It had two double bedrooms, one twin bedroom and two single bedrooms. There was also a bathroom and a shower room, kitchen and utility room and a large lounge-diner with a dining table and chairs. The house had many original period features such as sash windows, picture rails and ornate plaster work. Here they enjoyed each other's company as well as some privacy, which was particularly important to William, who felt he could relax now that his every movement was not being watched.

In an interview with a reporter from the Press Association, William later shone some light on life behind closed doors where he mucked in with the cooking and shopping. But although he tried his best he usually got himself into a mess in the kitchen and Kate would take over to save the day!

'I cook quite regularly for them and they cook for me, although we haven't had a house supper for quite a while because everyone's been doing exams and working quite hard,' he said. 'I've got some very good cooks in my house but I am absolutely useless. We tend to have chicken, curries and pasta. But we go out to eat quite a lot – whatever we feel like at the time.'

Their favourite haunts were the West Port Bar & Kitchen in the heart of town, The Doll's House restaurant and Ma Bells – a pub popular with students and located underneath The Golf Hotel. It was particularly lively at weekends with guest DJs and bands.

William told the Press Association reporter how he was enjoying the simple pleasures in life, things that he had never done before, such as shopping.

'I do a lot of shopping. I enjoy shopping, actually,' he said. 'I get very carried away, you know, just food shopping. I buy lots of things and then I go back to the house and see the fridge is full of all the stuff I've just bought.

'I like cinemas, bars, restaurants and lots of sport – on the beach, playing quick golf – just making use of everything up here. There is quite a lot to do.'

Like many student households the early intention of domesticated order had quickly deteriorated.

'We all get on very well and started off having rotas but, of course, it just broke down into complete chaos,' he said. 'Everyone helps out when they can. I try to help out when I can and they do the same for me. But, usually, you just fend for yourself.'

And he was throwing himself into sports at university. He had been voted polo captain (perhaps not surprisingly), and had taken to swimming and also participating in rugby tournaments as well as football on Sundays. He had been playing hockey but had stopped after a friend of his had his teeth knocked out! 'It put me off a bit,' he admitted.

In late November 2002, William invited a group of close friends to a shooting party at Wood Farm on the Sandringham estate – the Queen's country residence in Norfolk. They included Olivia Bleasdale, Virginia Fraser and Kate. By this stage the friends acknowledged William and Kate as a 'couple' and at Sandringham they often walked off on their own. The group slept in a six-bedroom cottage on the estate and enjoyed relaxing in each other's company.

Back at St Andrews, Kate and William attended the May Ball organised by the university's Kate Kennedy Club. The event was held in marquees in the grounds of Craigtoun Country Park, two miles from the centre of the town. A few weeks later Kate excitedly watched William playing in a rugby tournament.

During the summer break, Kate belatedly celebrated her 21st birthday in a marquee in the garden of her parents' house in Bucklebury, Berkshire, in June. As guests, including friends from St Andrews and Marlborough, sipped champagne, everyone was awaiting the arrival of Prince William. But it was to be a low-key and brief visit. He slipped in quietly without any fuss and, after having greeted Kate and met her parents and family members, he departed early – long before the sit-down meal and dancing commenced – to be driven back to Highgrove.

The following week William held his own 21st birthday celebration at Windsor Castle and Kate was invited. The party theme was 'Out of Africa' and the 300 guests, including the Royal Family, wore African attire. Giant elephant statues and animal skins were brought in, tribal masks were worn, an African band played and African food was on the menu.

Kate was overwhelmed by the grandeur of this captivating Royal residence that the Queen regards as her 'home', but distinctly underwhelmed to find that seated in pride of place beside William at the dinner table was another girl – Jessica 'Jecca' Craig.

William had met Jecca when he had gone to Africa on a school

LEFT: Catherine staying cool at the Game Fair at Blenheim Palace, August 2004.

trip in 1988. He went to the stunning Lewa Downs in Kenya to visit a game reserve owned by Jecca's conservationist father.

Pretty, with long blonde hair, she had attracted the Prince's attention and they had stayed in touch. But if Kate was concerned, she didn't show it. Instead, she played it rather cool. And back at St Andrews in September, Kate and William's relationship became distinctly warmer…

The Hope Street housemates moved to a more rural location, which suited William. It was a spacious stone cottage called Balgove House, about a mile west of the town at Strathtyrum, a sprawling private estate owned by wealthy 22-year-old landowner Henry Cheape, whose family are friends of the Royal Family.

With open countryside to walk in without being seen by others and warming open fires back home inside the cottage, it proved to be the ideal retreat for William and Kate to relax in each other's company and to get to know each other better.

Kate was also invited by William to spend some weekends with him at Highgrove, where she was introduced to Prince Charles. Other weekend breaks were spent at Birkhall, Prince Charles's retreat near Balmoral.

But this quiet and idyllic romance was about to attract the full blare of publicity…

CHAPTER THREE

THE SECRET'S OUT

The university students and local residents at St Andrews had been remarkably discrete in keeping the growing romance between William and Kate a secret. And the press, on their best behaviour in the light of criticism regarding the 'hounding' of the late Princess Diana, were still striving to give William his privacy and not to respond to rumours about the romance.

But one report of a 'romance' did leak – in the Daily Telegraph. The newspaper article said that it was 'an open secret that he [William] had had a fairly serious fling' with Jecca Craig during his gap-year in Kenya two years earlier.

In the interview for the Press Association just prior to his 21st birthday, William had categorically denied that he had a girlfriend.

'There's been a lot of speculation about every single girl I'm with and it actually does quite irritate me after a while, more so because it's a complete pain for the girls,' he said.

'These poor girls, you know, who I've either just met and get photographed with, or they're friends of mine, suddenly get thrown into the limelight and their parents get rung up and so on. I think it's a little unfair on them really.

'I'm used to it because it happens quite a lot now. But it's very difficult for them and I don't like that at all. I don't have a steady girlfriend.'

Enlarging on the difficulty he faced with girls and relationships, he explained, 'If I fancy a girl and I really like her and she fancies me back, which is rare, I ask her out. But at the same time, I don't want to put them in an awkward situation because a lot of people don't quite understand what comes with knowing me, for one, and secondly, if they were my girlfriend, the excitement it would probably cause.'

He then modestly joked, 'Only the mad girls chase me, I think. No, I've never been aware of anyone chasing me but if there were, could they please leave their telephone number.'

That April, Kate joined William on Prince Charles's traditional skiing holiday to Klosters in Switzerland. Charles was there once more with his regular skiing companion Patty Palmer-Tomkinson. Also amongst the group was Harry Legge-Bourke, the brother of William's former nanny Tiggy Legge-Bourke; William's old pal Guy Pelly; another friend of his named William van Cutsem, whose father Hugh owns an estate near Sandringham, and his girlfriend Katie James.

The occasion always attracted the press and, perhaps in a deliberate move to bring Kate from out of the shadows, there was no

PREVIOUS SPREAD: William and Catherine return to their old university, February 2011.

LEFT: Catherine in Kuala Lumpur during her visit to Malaysia with William, September 2012.

effort to keep her away from William on the slopes.

A photograph of the smiling couple, wearing red and black salopettes and ski-jackets, duly appeared in the *Sun* newspaper on 1 April 2004. He was looking down at her tenderly and neither was making any attempt to hide their love from the public gaze.

Kate was suddenly thrown into the spotlight with the media speculating about the romance, researching her family background and debating whether she might one day be Queen. Amidst all this commotion, the pair returned to St Andrews and tried to focus on their studies.

The secret may have turned into public knowledge but Kate was now more cautious in being seen with William, mindful of yet more 'intimate' photographs finding their way into newspapers. So, unlike before when she had supported William as he took part in a rugby sevens competition, playing for the Westport Bar team, she did not turn up.

However she was less guarded the following month when she accompanied him to that year's May Ball at Kinkell Farm, which that year had a 'saints and sinners' theme. They cut a dash on the dance floor and chatted and laughed into the early hours before making their way home.

Towards the end of May William took part in a photo-shoot on the farmland at Highgrove and told the press that his career after university was likely to be in the armed forces.

'There has been a lot of speculation,' he said. 'I've not made any serious plans yet, but the armed forces would be the best move at the moment. I really value all the efforts and professionalism of those guys. Soldiering is a risky business and there are a lot of guys out there risking their lives for us. I haven't decided anything yet. I just want to concentrate on graduating at the moment.'

Within a few months the press, who had only just proclaimed the Royal Romance, were speculating that it was all over. It wouldn't be the first time that such stories would appear. There were rumours that William was going back to Africa that summer to reunite with Jecca Craig. It proved to be unfounded as William didn't go. Instead, he and Kate, along with six other friends, flew out to Rodrigues Island, near Mauritius in the Indian Ocean, for a two-week summer holiday

William had spent part of his gap-year here in 2000 and had been eager to return. In this sun-kissed paradise island they donned

wetsuits to go scuba diving and William hired a motorbike, which he enjoyed riding along the beach road.

Within days of flying home, William was on his travels again, this time meeting up with an old friend, Texan heiress Anna Sloan, for a week's holiday on her family's ranch in Nashville in the United States. This again prompted speculation that all was not well between William and Kate.

But later that year William and Kate attended a high-profile ball at the Dunhill Links pro-am golf tournament where golf-playing celebrities included Hollywood actors Michael Douglas, Dennis Hopper and Kevin Costner. William took to the dance floor with Jemima Khan at one stage before being joined by Kate and some university friends.

The only slippery slope in sight was a skiing trip. They went on two in the early months of 2005. First was a long weekend in the Swiss resort of Verbier at the end of February, with half a dozen friends. This was followed by Klosters the following month. Here, Kate bonded with Prince Charles and was relaxed in his company. She also joked with Prince Harry.

William and Harry were the focus of attention from the gathered press at first but it was Prince Charles who was ultimately to hit headlines around the world after he made an unfortunate gaffe …

On the first night of their holiday, William, Harry, Kate and friends, including Guy Pelly, enjoyed après ski drinking and dancing into the early hours at Casa Antica nightclub where his mother, Princess Diana, had danced the night away with friends in 1987 while Charles remained at the chalet watching a video. William also spoke to reporters about his father's forthcoming marriage to Camilla Parker Bowles on 9 April – and also of his own marriage prospects.

'Look, I'm only 22 for God's sake. I'm too young to marry at my age. I don't want to get married until I'm at least 28 or maybe 30.'

And he took the opportunity to thank the media for the way they had been behaving during his time at university at St Andrews.

'I really mean it when I say we are both very grateful to the media for the way they have allowed us a degree of space. It meant a great deal to me that I was able to study and live a relatively normal life at St Andrews.'

Hours later, a slightly worse-for-wear William and Harry joined their father on the slopes for a traditional press photo-call. Flanked by his sons and placing his hands on their shoulders, Charles looked grumpy. He commented to William in a low-voice, which was picked up by microphones and heard by television viewers, 'What do we do?' William replied, 'Keep smiling.'

When the BBC's royal correspondent, Nicholas Witchell, asked how he was feeling in the run-up to his wedding to Camilla, he replied, 'It's a very nice thought, isn't it? I'm very glad you've heard of it, anyway.' Then he was clearly heard to mutter to his sons, 'Bloody people. I can't bear that man. He's so awful, he really is.'

It was a PR disaster but fortunately the perfect antidote was close at hand – a Royal wedding. Such occasions have the ability to put a smile on the faces of even the most cynical and jaded members of the public. And it was just the lift that Charles needed at that time.

More than 20,000 people cheered as the Charles and Camilla arrived at Windsor's Guildhall for their small, private civil wedding. Afterwards, they returned to Windsor Castle for a service of blessing led by the Archbishop of Canterbury. About 800 of the couple's family and friends attended including the Queen and Prince Philip. But Kate had not been invited.

After the ceremony, the couple walked around and chatted to members of the public gathered outside the chapel. They then made their way to a reception, hosted by the Queen, at the castle's State Apartments.

Back at St Andrews a few days later, William took part in a seven-a-side football tournament and Kate and some girl pals turned out to cheer him on. She showed a willingness to tuck into traditional football supporters food when she wolfed down a hamburger from a fast-food van.

After finishing their final exams, William and Kate embarked on a month-long restful break at Balmoral at the end of May 2005, enjoying long walks amidst the hills and indulging in a spot of fishing.

But the start of June saw a tricky encounter for Kate when she accompanied William to the wedding of his friend, Hugh van Cutsem, to Rose Astor, with the Prince acting as usher. Also there was Jecca Craig.

She turned heads in an unusual, eye-catching, large, brown cowboy hat and poncho as she turned up for the church service in Burford, Oxfordshire with a male friend. Kate was more traditionally dressed in a white jacket and black hat.

With their student days behind them, it was now time to say farewell to St Andrews, where they had fallen in love, at the

TOP: Catherine grabs a burger while watching William playing in a rugby sevens tournament in St Andrews, April 2005.

BOTTOM: William playing rugby in St Andrews, April 2005.

graduation ceremony on 23 June. Kate's proud parents, Michael and Carole, mingled with the others on the lawns of Lower College Hall, outside St Salvator's, enjoying strawberries and champagne. Also in attendance were Prince Charles, Camilla and the Queen and Duke of Edinburgh.

When it was time to move into Younger Hall for the ceremony, everyone took their seats, with Kate five rows in front of William. One by one, students' names were called and they knelt in front of the university chancellor's wooden pulpit where the chancellor, Sir Kenneth Dover, tapped their heads with a small, 17th century scarlet cloth cap said to contain a fragment from the trousers of the religious reformer John Knox. They then headed to an anteroom to collect their parchment. Kate received a 2:1 Hons in the History of Art and William a 2:1 in Geography.

Kate, dressed in a white blouse and short, black skirt under her black gown, smiled broadly as she returned to her seat. And the Queen's face lit up when it was William's turn.

At the end of the ceremony, principal and vice-chancellor Dr Brian Lang, made the poignant remark to students, 'You will have made lifelong friends. You may have met your husband or wife. Our title as the top matchmaking university in Britain signifies so much that is good about St Andrews, so we rely on you to go forth and multiply.'

Following the ceremony, William told reporters, 'Today is a very special day for me and I am delighted that I can share it with my family, and in particular with my grandmother, who has made such an effort to come, having been under the weather.

'I have thoroughly enjoyed my time at St Andrews and I shall be very sad to leave. I just want to say a big thank you to everyone who has made my time here so enjoyable. I have been able to lead as normal a student life as I could have hoped for and I'm very grateful to everyone, particularly the locals, who have helped make this happen.'

A chapter had ended and a new one was about to begin.

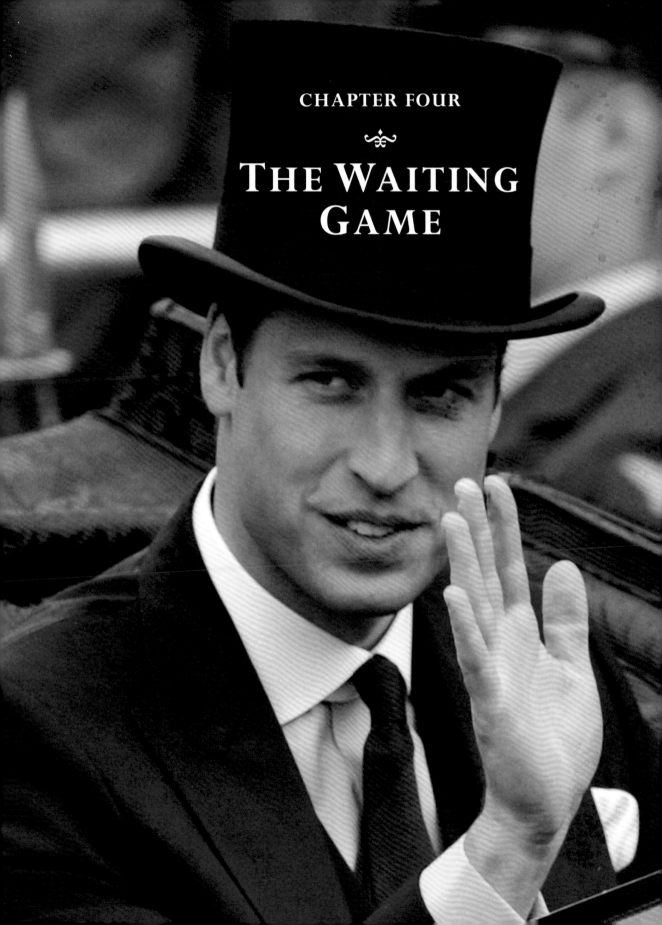

CHAPTER FOUR

THE WAITING GAME

There had been rumours that William and Kate had split up when they went their own ways after university. But they were quelled with a very public display of affection as the couple were watched a polo match at the Beaufort Polo Club near Highgrove in June 2005. She held his hand and was seen to stroke his face as they watched the final of the Argentine Cup. Kate giggled as she pointed her mobile phone at him to take his picture. Later he walked off and returned with an ice cream for her.

They seemed to be making the most of their time together before being apart for much of the coming summer. The following week William would be flying to New Zealand to carry out official Royal duties, followed by trips to Africa, the United States, Spain, Portugal and India.

While Kate remained at home with her parents in Berkshire, William represented the Queen in New Zealand at events commemorating the 60th anniversary of the end of the Second World War. But he also spent some time hanging out with the touring British Lions rugby team, joining them in training and watching some of their matches.

He laid a wreath of poppies in Wellington and went on a walkabout to say hello to the crowds of people watching. He also visited a children's hospital and played volleyball with some delighted pupils at a boys' high school.

At the end of a successful trip, he flew to Kenya to meet up with Jecca Craig at her family's nature reserve. But this time Kate was going too, along with some other of their mutual friends. During the day they helped out on the reserve and later spent romantic evenings in a wooden lodge, watching the stars.

They flew back from Kenya a few weeks later but William's royal commitments kept him away from Kate for much of the remaining summer months. In September, he joined the Queen and the Duke of Edinburgh at the annual Braemar Gathering in Aberdeenshire, where a large crowd of spectators enjoyed the spectacle of the Highland Games.

The following month he spent four days at the Royal Military Academy Sandhurst in order that the army might assess his suitability to become an officer. The tests involved a work-out in the gym, a gruelling series of physical challenges on the assault course, a series of written tests on general knowledge, army history and current affairs and finally a series of interviews with army top brass.

PREVIOUS SPREAD: William and Catherine in a carriage during the Queen's Diamond Jubilee celebrations, June 2012.

TOP: The lounge area of the lodge where William and Catherine stayed in Kenya, July 2005.

BOTTOM: One of the lodge's bedrooms, July 2005.

Kate was now dividing her time between her flat in London, that her parents had bought for her, and the family home in Berkshire.

In November she managed to meet up with William for a meal in London before meeting her mum, Carole, at a Christmas shopping exhibition at Olympia.

William passed his officer's tests at Sandhurst with flying colours. He would be joining the military academy in January 2006 to begin his officer training. Harry was already there. But first William was to undertake some work experience at HSBC bank. He spent a week at the company's charities branch near Clarence House but when he moved to the investment division at offices in Canary Wharf, East London, he got a taste of what life was like for long-suffering commuters when he got stuck in a traffic jam on his first day and was an hour late for work!

Spending so much time apart again gave rise to rumours of a split. And it was to be a direct question from a towering All Blacks rugby player during a team visit to meet the Royal Family at Buckingham Palace that was to give the world an update on his relationship with Kate.

When Ali Williams, who had met William on his visit to New Zealand earlier that summer, asked William how his relationship with Kate was progressing, William was momentarily startled by his bluntness but replied, that it was 'going well. Going steady.' The story appeared in the following day's newspapers.

After his stint at HSBC William spent time at RAF Valley on the island of Anglesey, North Wales, learning more about the work of the base's mountain rescue team, and enjoying a trip in one of their training jets. That Christmas he spent with the rest of his family in the traditional festive retreat at the Queen's estate in Sandringham, Norfolk, while Kate spent it with her own family. But she joined him briefly in Sandringham in the New Year before they flew out for a long weekend to Klosters. With William about to embark on a 44-week training schedule at Sandhurst the pair knew that they would not be seeing much of each other in the year ahead so they made the most of their time in Klosters, preferring to spend evenings together in a friend's chalet rather than going out to bars.

On the third day there, they openly kissed in the public glare while on the slopes, proving they were very much in love. The following day they flew back home and enjoyed a night out with friends at a French bistro in Mayfair as a way of saying farewell

TOP: Catherine and Pippa in the Royal Box for the presentation of the trophies at the Wimbledon Men's Singles Final, when Roger Federer beat Andy Murray, July 2012.

BOTTOM: Murray fan Catherine watching him play the previous year at Wimbledon, June 2011.

TOP LEFT: Catherine
flashes her trademark smile
during a visit to Liverpool,
February 2012.

TOP RIGHT: William and
Catherine greeting the
crowds during a trip to
Cambridge, November
2012.

BOTTOM: Catherine
samples a smoothie
cocktail called 'The
Duchess' at The Brink
alcohol-free bar in
Liverpool, February 2012.

before William started his army officer training.

A few days later he drove to Sandhurst with Prince Charles where they were greeted by Major General Andrew Ritchie. William settled into the dormitory with the other recruits and into a routine of training, drills, kit inspections and boot polishing.

Early in February he had a weekend break, meeting up with Kate at Highgrove and unwinding over a drink at a nearby pub, The Tunnel House, with his cousin Zara, her brother Peter Phillips and Guy Pelly. On Monday he returned to Sandhurst, while Kate went back to her parents.

But she was to make a notable appearance in March at the Cheltenham Gold Cup, where she mixed with members of the Royal Family for the first time without Prince William by her side. This was seen as a sign that she was becoming increasingly accepted into the Royal Family, although the nation was longing for a proposal! She looked elegant in a three-quarter length cream fitted coat by Katherine Hooker with brown boots and a brown, fur Cossack-style hat. Later she joined Prince Charles and Camilla for lunch in the royal enclosure.

The following day she met up with William at Eton College in Windsor, as he took some leave to take part in an old boys' Eton Field Game match – a game unique to the school which is a mix of football and rugby.

After the game, Kate confidently walked onto the pitch to kiss her prince on the cheek and also playfully ruffled his thinning hair.

After three months training William began his Easter holidays on 12 April. He enjoyed a night out drinking at a private members club in central London with Kate and his brother, Harry, to celebrate Harry having completed his officer training. Two weeks later, William and Kate flew out for a week's holiday in Mustique – the favourite holiday isle of Princess Margaret in the 1960s.

William and Kate stayed with some friends in a cliff-top villa that belonged to the owners of the Jigsaw fashion chain and commanded breath-taking views over the sea. They returned home on 6 May for the wedding of William's stepsister, Laura Parker Bowles, the following day in Wiltshire.

In June they attended the Boodles Boxing Ball at the Royal Lancaster Hotel in London, a charity event whose organisers include William's friend Hugh van Cutsem. The society black-tie evening begins with a champagne reception, dinner and an auction to raise money for the Starlight Foundation, a charity that grants the wishes of terminally ill children. After that comes the boxing in which the amateur contestants are drawn from high society.

Described by founder and organizer James Amos, the director of jewellers Boodles, as 'an event put on by friends for friends,' Hugh van Cutsem was amongst those who bravely slugged it out in the ring over three rounds and was victorious on the night.

Kate wore a striking blue BCBG Max Azria gown and happily cheered and applauded the boxers.

Yet this was a strange time for Kate. She was living an odd life, trying to find some semblance of normality, but always feeling like she was in limbo. One moment she was mixing with royalty and enjoying intimate moments with a Prince and the next she was pushing a trolley around a supermarket with mum, Carole, helping to do the weekly shop. At other times she would hop on and off a bus in London whilst clothes shopping.

In September 2006 William and Kate flew out to the holiday isle of Ibiza where they chartered a yacht with some friends, before William started his third and final term at Sandhurst.

Kate, still wondering what the future held for her, finally decided to get a job. She contacted John and Belle Robinson, the husband and wife founders of Jigsaw, and began working for them at their London headquarters for four days a week as an accessories buyer.

In early December she joined William and other members of the Royal Family at Sandringham and watched William in a pheasant shoot he had organised for friends. Rosy-cheeked and smiling with her long hair blowing in the breeze, she looked very at home and happy.

A few days later she was proudly watching William at his passing out parade at Sandurst, sitting with her parents with a broad smile on her face and excitedly pointing at her dashing officer boyfriend as he marched past.

She wore a red coat over a black dress and a wide brimmed black hat and gloves. Sitting nearby was the Queen, Prince Philip, Prince Charles and Camilla. William was now Second Lieutenant Wales in the Blues and Royals, the regiment in which Harry was already serving, which, along with the Life Guards, make up the Household Cavalry.

William would next undertake a four-month course at Bovington Camp, Dorset, to train as a troop commander in an armoured reconnaissance unit.

TOP: Catherine in the National Orchid Garden at the Singapore Botanic Gardens, September 2012.

BOTTOM: From the day she became engaged, Catherine grew accustomed to receiving flowers and chatting to large crowds.

But their long periods of separation began to take their toll as William focussed on his officer's life and Kate continued working at Jigsaw.

When they attended the opening day of the Cheltenham races at the end of March 2007, Kate appeared to be her usual smiling self but William seemed a little glum and at one point he walked several paces ahead of her, with his head down and his hands deep in his pockets.

Kate, who was fast becoming a style-icon, wore a fitted, brown, tweed jacket and matching knee-length skirt over a pale blue, open-necked blouse. On Gold Cup Day she wore a powder blue jacket sporting large black buttons and black piping over a fitted, open-necked, white blouse, teamed with a brown knee-length skirt, brown Philip Treacy beret and paisley scarf.

It seemed that all was not well in her relationship with William. A few days later he was training in Dorset and Kate saw little of him over the next few weeks. But unfortunately she was able to read about him....

On a night out in Bournemouth with fellow officers, they let hair down at various bars before ending up in a nightclub. When a couple of teenage girls there subsequently sold their stories to the newspapers about how the officers were flirting with them, it sparked renewed gossip that the royal romance was over. And this time it was more than just gossip.

With their relationship severely strained, William suggested to a heartbroken Kate that they take a break from each other.

CHAPTER FIVE

❧

THE SINGLE
LIFE

Kate retreated to her family home in Berkshire. She had been given a week off from working at Jigsaw and she seemed set to withdraw from her high-profile life.

Yet she was determined not to hide herself away and mope for long. She wanted to get on with her life – without or without her prince – and a few days later she drove to her flat in Chelsea to pick up her racquet for a game of tennis.

She also went out partying with friends until the early hours of the morning at Mahiki nightclub in Mayfair, where William had partied with his pals a few days earlier. It seemed a deliberate choice of venue designed to let everyone, including the Prince, know that she was an independent girl, enjoying the single life and the freedom to dance and party with friends whenever and wherever she pleased.

A week later and she was out on the town again, enjoying lunch with some girl friends at a Thai restaurant in Chelsea before going onto another favourite venue of William's, Boujis nightclub.

That April she was approached by her friend Alicia Fox-Pitt, who was with her at Marlborough College, to join the Sisterhood. It was a group of fun and adventure-seeking women who were to attempt to cross the English Channel from Dover to Cap Gris Nez, near Calais, in a dragon boat, racing against a team of men, to raise money for charity.

Kate jumped at the chance to join them. It was just the kind of physical pursuit she enjoyed and an ideal distraction at this difficult emotional time in her life. She began training with them in earnest three times a week on the River Thames at Chiswick and Putney. There was to be a crew of 19 with two extras in reserve for the crossing with the event due to take place in August. Kate's job was a standing one, as helmsman, steering the tiller and shouting instructions as the others paddled.

One of the crew explained that Kate's job was demanding. 'It might look easy, but being on the tiller is hard,' she said. 'It's like standing on a wobble board the whole time and because you have to do all the shouting, you cannot relax at all. On the paddles you can switch off a bit more.'

Kate's involvement attracted many newspaper photographers. Pictures of her in her wet-suit, smiling and ruddy-cheeked were all over the press. She looked the picture of health, as if she did not have a care in the world.

By the end of May, Kate's younger sister, Pippa, had finished her

PREVIOUS SPREAD: Pippa and Catherine on their way home after a night out in London, October 2007.

TOP: Catherine's family home in Bucklebury, Berkshire, to where she retreated after splitting with William, spring 2007.

BOTTOM: Catherine jumped at the chance to train with the Sisterhood team for a cross-channel dragon boat race, April 2007.

final exams at Edinburgh University where she earned a degree in English Literature, and had moved to London. Kate was pleased to see her and, with Prince William now out of her life, the two sisters, who had always got along well, spent a lot of time together, including a girly night out at Boujis.

Kate's calculated 'carefree' attitude was working because, William, still training in Dorset, was starting to realise what he was missing. Out of the blue he contacted Kate and asked if they could meet up at his apartment in Clarence House on 26 May to talk things over.

Kate agreed but she was not about to drop everything and rush back into his arms. Instead, in an exquisitely guileful move, she made him feel even more uncomfortable when she was back at Mahiki a few days later, arriving on the arm of shipping heir Henry Ropner, who had gone to school with William at Eton and who had dated Jecca Craig. And she left the night club with another man, making no attempt to avoid the waiting paparazzi. The following day the newspapers carried pictures calling him a 'mystery male friend.' He turned out to be just a friend of both Kate and William's, but Kate was continuing to underline that she was now free to do as she pleased.

The couple's heart-to-heart at Clarence House must have gone well because on 9 June Kate travelled to Dorset to accompany William to a lively mess party at his barracks to celebrate the end of his course. They took to the dance floor and looked like their old, happy selves once more.

But Kate, who had never given up hope of them getting back together, continued to play things her way and it was to prove to be a master class in winning back your man!

A few days later, back in London, she was out partying with friends again, this time at Raffles nightclub. And on 17 June she flew out to Ibiza for a holiday with friends, including her brother James and Emilia d'Erlanger, a friend from Marlborough College and St Andrews.

In the meantime, there was speculation in the press about whether or not Kate would be attending the high-profile Concert for Diana at Wembley Stadium on 1 July. The concert was the brainchild of Princes William and Harry to celebrate what would have been their mother's 46th birthday and commemorate Princess Diana's death, with the 10th anniversary of the fateful Paris car crash coming at the end of August.

The line-up of musical acts included favourites of Diana's such as

TOP: Pippa and Catherine shopping in Chelsea, July 2007.

BOTTOM: The sisters at a book launch in Bond Street, May 2007.

Duran Duran and Sir Elton John, along with more contemporary acts of the time like Kanye West, P Diddy and Joss Stone.

The day before the concert, Kate had been at Wimbledon watching Maria Sharapova playing. It later transpired that she had spent that night at Clarence House with William. The following day she was, indeed, at the concert, sitting in the royal box but kept everyone guessing about the state of her relationship with William because while he was seated in the front row with Harry and his girlfriend Chelsy Davy, she was sitting two rows behind with William's friend Thomas van Straubenzee.

But both William and Kate were in high spirits. He laughingly participated in a 'Mexican wave' with the rest of the crowd and Kate sang along enthusiastically to Take That performing '(I want you) Back For Good'.

But it was a different story at the after-show VIP party where William and Kate took to the dance floor and shared a kiss. It was to leave no one in any doubt that their relationship was very much back on.

CHAPTER SIX

WILL HE...
WON'T HE?

The day after the Concert for Diana and after-show party, Kate was back at Wimbledon enjoying the tennis between Robin Soderling and Rafael Nadal on Court Number One. She looked happy and in high spirits as she cheered on the players and chatted and laughed with a female friend.

Three weeks later and she was very much back in the royal fold when she attended the Duchess of Cornwall's 60th birthday banquet at Highgrove. Camilla has always been fond of Kate and took her under her wing at an early stage, so she was delighted that she was back with William.

Prince Harry and his girlfriend, Chelsy, were away on holiday but Kate, dressed in an elegant ivory gown, was at ease as she sipped cocktails with Zara Phillips and her England international rugby player boyfriend Mike Tindall in the gardens. Princess Anne and her husband, Vice-Admiral Timothy Laurence, were there along with the Earl and Countess of Wessex. The many celebrity guests included Stephen Fry, Dame Judy Dench, Edward Fox, Sir David Frost, Joanna Lumley, Timothy West and his actress wife Prunella Scales.

A three-course organic meal was followed by dancing. William playfully sang along to a recording of Frank Sinatra's 'It Had To Be You', as he gazed intently to a giggling Kate on the dance floor.

Now firmly re-established with William, Kate pulled out of the Sisterhood and the dragon boat cross-channel race which took place on 24 August. A week earlier William and Kate shared a romantic holiday on the idyllic island of Desroches in the Indian Ocean. For a change they went alone, without friends and stayed in the luxurious Desroches Island Resort, overlooking a clear blue lagoon, booking in under the names of Martin and Rosemary.

Here they enjoyed scuba diving, strolling along the brilliant white sands, fringed with palm trees and dined in the restaurants at night. Back home in the UK there was some speculation in the newspapers that this beautiful island would be the perfect place for the Prince to propose.

But as romantic as the holiday was, a marriage proposal was not forthcoming. And the wait would go on far longer than anyone expected.

Back in London, the couple continued to visit familiar haunts such as Mahiki and Boujis nightclubs. But on one visit to Boujis in October, just days after the start of the inquest into the death of Princess Diana in a fatal crash while being followed by photographers,

William complained of being 'aggressively' chased in their car by paparazzi after leaving the venue.

A Clarence House spokesman said, 'Prince William was concerned by the threatening behaviour of the paparazzi in London. Having already been photographed leaving the club, he and Kate Middleton were then pursued in his car by photographers on motorcycles, in vehicles and on foot. The aggressive pursuit was potentially dangerous and worrying for them. It seems incomprehensible, particularly at this time, that this behaviour is still going on.'

In mid-October they spent the weekend at Birkhall, on the edge of the Balmoral estate, where they often used to stay when students at St Andrews. William and Kate had startled fellow airplane passengers when they boarded a scheduled British Airways flight from Gatwick to Aberdeen. At Birkhall they were joined by Prince Charles and Camilla for the deerstalking season. Active Kate dressed in camouflage and was shown by two ghillies how to lie on the floor in wait, with a hunting rifle ready.

The following month she and Pippa went to a Halloween party at Mahiki with Kate dressed as a rather beguiling 'witch', in a black mini-dress and cape with knee-length black boots.

But as she waited for a proposal from her prince, Kate put her mind to focussing on doing something with her life, away from the royal circle. Her thoughts turned towards becoming a photographer and maybe opening a gallery. She quit Jigsaw at the beginning of November to pursue this goal.

Later that month, she joined a group of young royals to celebrate the 30th birthday of Princess Anne's son, Peter Phillips. The gang, including William, Harry, Zara Phillips and Prince Andrew's daughters Beatrice and Eugenie, enjoyed a restaurant meal in central London before going on to Volstead nightclub in Mayfair.

At the end of November, Kate staged her first photography exhibition, featuring a project by Alistair Morrison, who had met Kate when she was studying History of Art at St Andrew's. Dressed in a figure-hugging charcoal dress, Kate was joined by her parents and Pippa at the gallery in London's Chelsea. Alistair Morrison had persuaded celebrities such as Tom Cruise, Ewan McGregor, Sting and Catherine Zeta Jones to have their photographs taken in a special photo-booth he had set up. The collated photographs were put into a book with proceeds from sales going to the international children's charity UNICEF.

RIGHT: Catherine on the morning of her 25th birthday, enduring the attentions of the press, January 2007.

Prince William arrived late, wearing a stripy shirt and blazer and joined the Middletons for dinner after the event.

Alistair Morrison praised Kate's own ability behind the lens. 'She is very, very good, and it shows. She takes very beautiful, detailed photographs,' he said. 'She has such a huge talent and a great eye. I'm sure she will go far. She approached me when she was at university to come and do a little bit of work with her and we've kept in touch.'

In mid-December she was away from the glitz of London, looking every inch the countrywoman as she joined William on a pheasant shoot in Windsor Great Park. Wearing a brown jacket and fur hat, she followed in his wake, collecting the birds he had shot and throwing them into a game cart.

A few days later, as the Royal Family met up for Christmas at Sandringham, Kate headed off to the warmer climes of Barbados with her parents as well as Pippa and James. But she was back to celebrate the New Year with William at Highgrove before he was due to go on a four-month detachment with the RAF, starting at its training college at Cranwell, Lincolnshire, where he would be taught to fly a jet aircraft and a Squirrel helicopter. Over the next few months she would be seeing little of him as he would only get time away at weekends.

William missed Kate's 26th birthday celebration on 9 January 2008, which she spent with her parents and Pippa at a restaurant in Chelsea. Afterwards, the sisters went to Kitts Club in Sloane Square.

Kate had a military look about her in a double-breasted white coat with large, black buttons, fitted at the waist.

A few days later, with William still away training with the RAF, Kate was accompanied by two of his pals, Guy Pelly and Thomas van Straubenzee to the premiere of *Afrika! Afrika!* at the O2 Arena in London. The two-and-a-half hour show celebrates African culture and creativity with various artists and acts from African countries performing colourful, high-energy displays of dancing, acrobatics and singing.

After a month training at Cranwell, William transferred to RAF Linton-on-Ouse in North Yorkshire, where his flying tuition continued in a Tucano T1 training aircraft.

Kate was back in the company of Thomas van Straubenze when she attended the 2008 Cheltenham Cup in March. On Gold Cup Day she wore a short, navy-blue raincoat with a black trilby and matching scarf.

But she was reunited with William two days later when they took their fourth skiing trip to Klosters where Prince Charles joined them later in the week. Kate, in a white skiing jacket, was photographed playfully poking William with a ski pole.

After their holiday William was posted to RAF Shawbury, near Shrewsbury, Shropshire. He spent his final week at RAF Odiham, west of Basingstoke in Hampshire.

William had received criticism in the press for being allowed to fly a Chinook helicopter over his family home at Highgrove and for being given permission actually to land it at the Middleton home in Berkshire. He also used it to transport himself to the Scottish border town of Kelso to join Kate at the wedding of their close friend, Lady Iona Douglas-Home and banker Thomas Hewitt. His co-pilot flew the aircraft home. While his critics were scathing about this indulgence, others, including some in the RAF, pointed out that all pilots had to learn how to navigate accurately from point-to-point cross country and this was as good a way to train as any!

William received his RAF 'wings' from his proud father, Prince Charles, at RAF Cranwell on 11 April 2008. Kate, wearing the double-breasted, white coat she wore for her 26th birthday, proudly watched him at the ceremony, along with Camilla and Lady Sarah McCorquodale, the elder sister of Princess Diana. Charles, now Air Chief Marshal, had graduated from RAF Cranwell in 1971, when the ceremony was conducted by his father, the Duke of Edinburgh.

When William's name was called out he walked over to Charles and the pair smiled broadly at each other before Charles pinned on his 'wings' and shook his hand.

RAF Cranwell's commanding officer, Group Captain Nigel Wharmby, told the new pilots, 'To those who fly today, these badges are the most coveted of all our insignia and rightly so. To all the graduates, I say remember this day with great pride and enjoy it. You have most definitely earned it.'

Outside, the royal party looked at a display of historic aircraft but the strong wind and lashing rain curtailed the proceedings.

Four days later, Kate joined her family to celebrate her brother James's 21st birthday at a restaurant in central London. James had dropped out of university in Edinburgh, where he had been studying Environmental Resources Management, to set up his own offshoot of the family firm, the Cake Kit Company, which provided the ingredients and accessories for making novelty cakes. He was working at his parents' offices and staying at their home. Pippa, at this stage, was working for London-based events organiser Table Talk.

RIGHT: Attending the UK premier of Disneynature's *African Cats* in aid of the Tusk Trust charity of which William is patron, April 2012.

William flew out to the front line in Afghanistan on duty with the RAF at the end of April. Along with other officers, he brought home the body of a British trooper who had been killed in action. Then, taking leave from the RAF, he had a month-long break in May before starting an attachment to the Royal Navy at the beginning of June.

William took the opportunity to take part in a polo match with brother Harry at Coworth Park in Ascot, Berkshire and Kate joined Chelsy Davy in cheering on their boyfriends from the sidelines, both dressed similarly in short-fitted jackets, dark blue jeans with knee-high boots and sunglasses.

Although Kate had been at several functions where the Queen was also present, such as William's passing out parade at Sandhurst and graduation day at St Andrews, she had never been introduced to her. That was to change on 17 May when Kate joined the Queen, Prince Charles and the rest of the Royals at the wedding of the Queen's grandson Peter Phillips to Canadian-born Autumn Kelly at St George's Chapel in the grounds of Windsor Castle. Kate wore a pale-pink, fitted jacket, a black dress by her favourite fashion label, Issa (created by Brazilian designer, Daniella Helayel) teamed with a black pillbox hat and net veil.

William was far away, at Lewa Wilderness Lodge, Kenya, for the traditional Masai marriage ceremony of Batian Craig, the brother of Jecca, to Melissa Duveen.

Kate's appearance at the royal occasion, without William, was a major development which showed that the Royal Family was preparing for her to enter the inner ranks and it renewed gossip about how she would be the next royal bride. Although the Queen was naturally much occupied talking to her large family, she took the time to approach Kate and to say 'hello.' Kate was later to say that she thought the Queen was 'very friendly.'

Four days after the wedding, Kate flew out to Mustique to meet up with William for a holiday, staying on the east coast of the island at a hired villa in the cliffs above Macaroni Beach. The villa has its own swimming pool, bar, tennis court, games room and private footpath down to the beach.

Having re-charged his batteries, William arrived at the Britannia Royal Naval College in Dartmouth at the start of June for a two-month attachment to the Royal Navy, where he would learn about seamanship, train alongside the Royal Marines and fly navy helicopters. His tour would also include time on board a destroyer.

On his first weekend off he travelled back to London to join
Kate as they attended that year's Boodles Boxing Ball at the Royal
Lancaster Hotel. Here, William and Kate met up with Harry and
Chelsy for a champagne reception, dinner and auction before joining
Guy Pelly, Thomas van Straubenzee, Jamie Murray Wells and Jecca
Craig in ringside seats for the boxing.

The Princes cheered on their friend James Meade who lost to Al
Poulain, a former equerry to Prince Charles. Jecca Craig was in the
corner of her boyfriend, Hugh Crossley, when he stepped into the
ring.

Kate, who caught attention by wearing an elegant, floor-length,
pink Issa gown with a plunging neckline, laughed, grimaced and,
at one point, hid her face behind her hands as the game boxers
exchanged blows. Impressed with the work that the Starlight
Foundation does, she later arranged for Party Pieces to donate party
bags to 10,000 sick children in hospitals over Christmas.

Later that month she watched William become a Knight of the
Garter in an ancient ceremony at St George's Chapel, Windsor.
Established by Edward III in 1348, the prestigious but archaic accolade
represents the highest order of chivalry and is in the Queen's personal
gifts, which she makes without advice from government ministers.

The origin of the Order of the Garter, whose symbol is a blue
'garter', is said to have derived from when King Edward attended
a ball in Calais at which Joan, Countess of Salisbury, accidentally
dropped her garter. Seeing her embarrassment, the King picked it up
and attached it to his own leg, announcing, 'Honi Soit Qui Mal Y
Pense,' meaning 'Evil be he that thinks evil of it.' It was to became
the motto of the order

But despite such a rich and noble history, Kate and Harry
couldn't manage to suppress a giggle as William walked past them,
dressed in the Order's blue velvet cape and ostrich-plumed cap.

Two days later and William was back at sea, spending 24 hours
underwater on the nuclear submarine, HMS *Talent*, taking part in an
exercise to track down and destroy an enemy submarine.

William celebrated his 26th birthday on 21 June and Kate spent the
weekend with him. They met up with Harry and Chelsy at the Beaufort
Polo Club in Gloucestershire to watch an England team play New
Zealand and later danced the night away in a marquee in the grounds.
Friends joined him for a birthday party held in the soundproof basement
bar at Highgrove, a favourite hang-out of both William and Harry's.

RIGHT: In Singapore,
Catherine and William
visited the Bay South
Garden, built on reclaimed
land, September 2012.

A couple of days later he took part in a two-month-long operation with the Royal Navy aboard the warship HMS *Iron Duke* to track down cocaine smugglers in Caribbean.

With William away and unable even to communicate a great deal with her, Kate attended various functions without him, including a musical tribute to celebrate Nelson Mandela's 90th birthday at Hyde Park in London, where acts such as Annie Lennox, Queen, Amy Winehouse and The Soweto Gospel Choir performed. And she went to her second royal wedding that year without William when Lady Rose Windsor, the youngest daughter of the Duke and Duchess of Gloucester, married George Gilman at the Queen's Chapel in St James's Palace. Kate wore a floaty, knee-length, floral dress and pale blue fitted jacket with a black feather fascinator

William and Kate were eventually reunited in Mustique towards the end of July. Now a firm favourite as a holiday destination with the couple, it was the third time they had stayed here. They settled in to a secluded villa on the west coast, overlooking the ocean. It has a swimming pool, cinema and a gym while the master bedroom has steps leading straight onto the beach.

In September, they flew out to Austria for the wedding of Chiara Hunt, the sister of their university friend Olivia, who married Rupert Evetts, a Blues and Royals officer, in Salzburg.

A week later there came some surprising news that Prince William, who was expected to return to the army, would instead be joining the RAF's search and rescue team as a Sea King helicopter pilot. He would quit the army in December and start training with the RAF in January.

William had come to love flying and working with the rescue team appealed to his natural instinct to want to help people and to do something useful in life. He also knew that, as third in line to the throne, his deployment to the front line in any conflict zone was not something the powers-that-be were ever likely to allow.

In a statement, the Prince said, 'It has been a real privilege to have spent the past year experiencing all aspects of the British Armed Forces. I now want to build on the training I have received to serve operationally, especially because, for good reasons, I was not able to deploy to Afghanistan this year with D Squadron of the Household Cavalry Regiment.

'Joining search and rescue is a perfect opportunity for me to serve in the Forces operationally, while contributing to a vital part of the country's emergency services.'

Many had expected that the Prince – whose military service was due to end in December – would take up full-time royal duties and marry the following year. Now a wedding looked a long way off.

From January 2009 he would start an intensive 18-month training period at RAF Kinross in Scotland and then move on to a three-year operational stint on Sea King helicopters, coping mostly with civilian emergencies across the country.

Meanwhile, Kate was involving herself in another charity fund-raising event. A childhood friend of hers, Tom Waley-Cohen, who was at Marlborough with her, had died at the age of 20 in July 2004 after a long battle against bone cancer. His family was raising funds for a surgical ward at Oxford Children's Hospital named after him. Kate, along with Tom's brother Sam – a businessman and amateur jockey who was a friend of hers – thought of a roller-disco to raise money for Tom's Ward along with a charity called Place2Be, which provides counselling to schoolchildren in need.

The Day-Glo Charity Roller Disco took place at the Renaissance Rooms in Vauxhall, South London and Kate wore a sequinned halter-neck top, bright yellow hotpants, pink leg-warmers and matching bracelet. Pippa also went, as did Princess Beatrice and Richard Branson's daughter Holly. Several times Kate fell over on the dance floor but she took it all in great spirits, laughing uproariously.

At the start of October it was William's turn to participate in a charity fund raiser. And this one was ideal for the motorbike loving Prince.

Like William, Prince Harry had a keen interest in South Africa and during his gap year in 2004, he had visited a centre for deaf children in Lesotho, meeting Prince Seeiso who told him about his country's many children who were the victims of poverty and the HIV/AIDS epidemic.

Two years later, Princes Harry and Seeiso set up a charity to help them, called Sentebale, which means 'Forget me not' in Sesotho.

Harry, who had caught the 'biking bug' from William, had formed the idea with his brother to combine charity with adventure in an eight-day motorbike ride across 1,000 miles of rough terrain through Africa from Port Edward on KwaZulu-Natal's southern coast down to Port Elizabeth.

The two brothers agreed to donate a minimum of £1,500 each to take part in the Enduro Africa 08 event, which would not only

RIGHT: Catherine with friend Sam Waley-Cohen at the Day-Glo Charity Roller Disco event, September 2008.

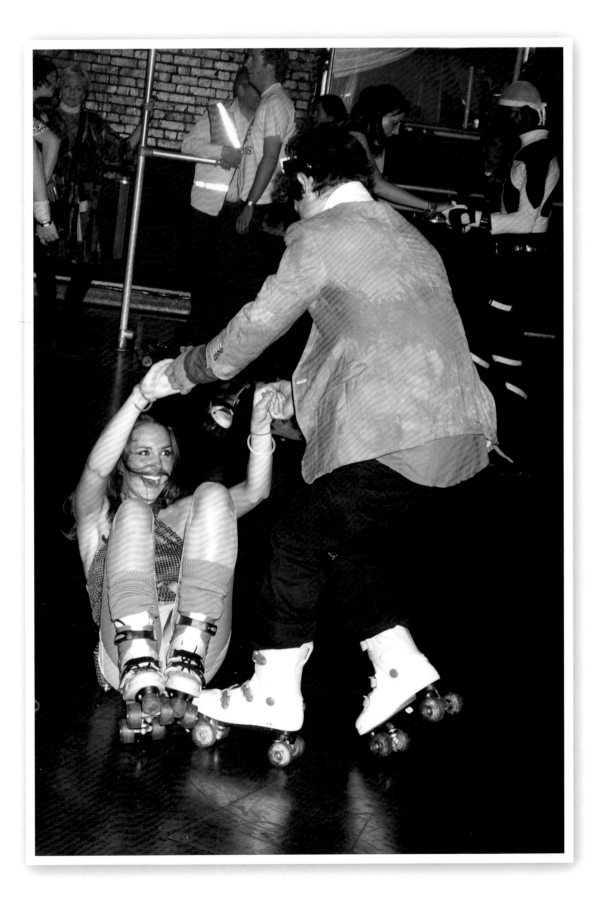

LEFT: Sam Waley-Cohen
helps to get Catherine back
on her wheels at the Day-
Glo Charity Roller Disco
event, September 2008.

raise money for Sentebale but also UNICEF and the Nelson Mandela
Children's Fund, both working in South Africa to either help
communities affected by AIDS or improve the prospects of youngsters.

Prince William described them as 'three absolutely brilliant
charities'.

The Princes were to travel in a group of around 10, meeting up
with other groups of fundraising bikers at the end of each day to swap
stories of their experiences and sleeping in modest accommodation.

Sitting on Honda CRF 230cc bikes just prior to setting off, William
and Harry, daubed with face paint, chatted to the assembled press.

Harry, a Household Cavalry officer, said that he was eagerly
looking forward to the trip. 'We never really spend any time
together. We've got separate jobs going on at the moment but it's
great fun. Well … I don't know yet, we'll have to tell you. We
might argue, we might have a bit of fun. We'll have to see how it
goes. But we're really looking forward to it.'

Asked about how much training they had done, William replied,
'Absolutely none whatsoever. We both ride bikes at the moment on
the road but on-road biking is completely different. All the off-road
stuff is up hill, down slopes, across rivers and is all rocky and hilly.'
The event was to raise over £300,000 for charity.

Away from her charity and photography work, Kate needed to
earn a living. But any job would have to be flexible so that she could
accompany Prince William in her 'limbo world' of being a semi
member of the royal family. And the easiest option open to her was
to return to working for the family business, Party Pieces, which she
did towards the end of the year, taking a technology course to learn
how to compile digital catalogues, photograph products and set up its
new venture, First Birthdays, which she was going to manage.

To mark his 60th birthday on 14 November 2008, Prince Charles
had two celebrations. The first was a formal one at Buckingham
Palace the evening before his actual birthday. Kate joined William
and other members of the Royal Family for a black-tie champagne
reception for 450 relatives, friends, charity officials, politicians and
several crowned heads of Europe.

At 7.30 p.m. the guests moved into the ballroom for a recital of
chamber music by the Philharmonia Orchestra, of which the prince
is patron. And after guests left at 9.00 p.m. the Royal Family moved
into the Queen's Gallery for a private dinner.

Two days later saw a far more informal 'bash' at Highgrove

where Rod Stewart sang many of his hit songs such as Maggie May and This Old Heart of Mine as Charles and Camilla were joined on the dance floor by William and Kate, Harry and Chelsy and other partygoers. Celebrities amongst the 250 guest included John Cleese, Dames Judy Dench and Maggie Smith, Stephen Fry, Joanna Lumley, Rowan Atkinson, Kenneth Branagh, Richard E Grant, Joan Rivers and Prunella Scales.

RIGHT: A portrait of Catherine in Lego, made by Lego artist Ed Diment, January 2012.

While aboard the warship HMS *Iron Duke* in the Caribbean, William had grown a bushy beard which Kate teased him about when they spent a weekend pheasant shooting at Sandringham in mid-December.

They spent Christmas apart, following royal protocol. Kate flew to Mustique, once more, this time with her family for a holiday, while William was with the Royal Family at Sandringham for their traditional celebrations. But the couple reunited at Birkhall for the New Year, with Prince Charles and Camilla. And they also spent Kate's birthday together on 9 January 2009, celebrating with a low-key family dinner at her parents' house.

William returned to at RAF Shawbury in Shropshire, where he had fallen in love with flying, on 11 January 2009 to begin 21 months of training as a search and rescue pilot. He swapped his RAF digs for a stone-built cottage nearby so that it would be more comfortable for Kate to stay when she visited.

In March he managed to get some time off to take Kate skiing for five days in the French Alps. That summer's holiday was spent once more in Mustique in August after William had been on attachment to RAF Valley in Anglesey, where he had first learnt about the work of the search and rescue team.

Kate combined her interests in charity and the arts when she held a fundraiser for the Starlight Children's Foundation at the Saatchi Gallery in London in October. Several well-known figures from the word of art and design were on hand to run a series of workshops to inspire and teach children how to be creative. The finished works were then sold at the gallery to raise money for the charity. Kate, accompanied by Prince William, wore an eye-catching, low-cut, grey halter-necked gown by Issa. England footballer Sol Campbell turned up and donated the football shirt and boots that he had worn when he played for Portsmouth in the 2008 FA Cup Final. And a Vivienne Westwood-designed rocking horse with safety pins on the saddle fetched £10,000 at the after-dinner auction.

Kate's parents, who also attended the £100-a-head, black-tie

TOP: Catherine shelters beneath a sunshade while visiting the Kranji War Memorial in Singapore, September 2012.

BOTTOM: William and Catherine arriving in Malau in the Solomon Islands, September 2012.

event, along with Pippa, donated a party for 20 youngsters as one of the evening's prizes.

The annual New Year retreat to Birkhall once more generated further gossip that this could just be the moment when Prince William proposed to Kate. But once more nothing happened!

A few days later she watched proudly as William was presented with a flying certificate and badge from his father, Prince Charles, after completing a year's advanced helicopter training course. But it was also an occasion for much amusement …

In his speech at the graduation ceremony at RAF Shawbury, Charles had everyone laughing when he made a humorous reference to William's future as a search and rescue pilot. He told the assembled graduates and their families, 'Some of you no doubt will find yourselves in Afghanistan where the ground troops will put great faith in you. Others no doubt among you will be plucking people from danger, maybe sheep in distress, not to mention endless ladies with conveniently sprained ankles on awkward mountainsides across the country.' William and Kate laughed heartily as he continued, 'Whatever the case, you will all be in charge of an amazingly expensive piece of kit that a lot of people won't want you to break, so I can only suggest you cultivate that sixth sense, if you know what I mean, which can so often keep you out of trouble. Today is a day, I think, of great pride for all of the parents, not to mention the girlfriends. We all know how hard our sons have worked in between all the other activities that we don't know about.'

Kate was delighted to be invited to Sandringham to spend her 28th birthday with William and the Queen. A couple of weeks later, Prince William went on a royal tour to Australia and New Zealand.

Marriage speculation increased once more when, during a 'walkabout' in Redfern, Australia, an elderly lady asked him when he would marry Kate. He smiled and replied, 'I keep saying – wait and see.'

March 2010 saw another skiing holiday for the couple, this time in the French resort of Courchevel, where they stayed in a luxury chalet with a group of friends, including Kate's sister, Pippa.

Back at RAF Valley, Anglesey, William had once more eschewed the officer's quarters to rent a cottage nearby where Kate regularly stayed with him for long weekends. It was to become a much-loved home for them in years to come, away from the limelight, perhaps invoking memories of the country cottage they shared whilst at St Andrews.

Their own wedding might not have been imminent, but William and Kate attended two friends' weddings in quick succession – both for old university colleagues. First was that of Emilia d'Erlanger in Devon at which Kate stole much of the attention in a bright red Issa dress. Two weeks later they made a nostalgic return to St Andrew's, where they had fallen in love, for the wedding of former university friend Oli Baker at St Salvator's Chapel. Kate wore an ivory brocade coat with a black pillbox hat for the ceremony.

That September saw William complete his helicopter training course at Anglesey where he was presented with his badge by the unit's commander, Group Captain Jonathan Dixon, in an informal ceremony at which the Prince had no guests.

'The course has been challenging, but I have enjoyed it immensely,' William said.

'I absolutely love flying, so it will be an honour to serve operationally with the Search and Rescue Force, helping to provide such a vital emergency service.'

He had joined 22 Squadron, C Flight as a co-pilot in a Sea King Mk3 helicopter covering Wales, western England and Northern Ireland and he would start his first operational shift the following month.

In October, William and Kate went back to Africa for a ten-day stay at Lewa Downs game reserve with some friends. Here, they managed to get away to spend some private time together and enjoy the breath-taking scenery which would leave special memories with them. They returned from Africa for another wedding, that of their friend, showjumper Harry Meade in Northleach, Gloucestershire. Kate looked radiant, dressed in a cobalt blue dress, black blazer and a wide-brimmed black hat, adorned with feathers. As they walked through the church porch she was all smiles as they shared a joke.

Royal wedding speculation hit fever pitch when it was learned that Kate's parents had stayed at Birkhall the following weekend, with Kate and William, where they took part in a private shooting party after ghillies showed them how to lie on the ground and aim a rifle.

Two weeks later came the announcement for which everyone had been waiting for …

LEFT: Catherine plants a tree at the opening of the Treehouse Hospice in Ipswich, March 2012.

RIGHT: Visiting Dulwich Picture Gallery to see an exhibition for the Prince's Foundation for Children and the Arts, March 2012.

CHAPTER SEVEN

WEDDING FEVER

The official statement from Clarence House on 16 November 2010, read: 'The Prince of Wales is delighted to announce the engagement of Prince William to Miss Catherine Middleton. The wedding will take place in the spring or summer of 2011, in London. Further details about the wedding day will be announced in due course. Prince William and Miss Middleton became engaged in October during a private holiday in Kenya. Prince William has informed the Queen and other close members of his family. Prince William has also sought the permission of Miss Middleton's father. Following the marriage, the couple will live in North Wales, where Prince William will continue to serve with the Royal Air Force.'

While in Africa with friends, William had led Kate out of Lewa Downs wildlife park to a romantic spot by a lake on the slopes of Mount Kenya. Here, where they had some privacy, with a backdrop of snowy peaks and a spectacular view, he had proposed. And he presented her with his mother's engagement ring – the famous oval, 18-carat, blue sapphire surrounded by 14 diamonds.

Prince Charles said he was 'thrilled, obviously' about the engagement, but couldn't resist joking, 'They've been practising long enough!'

Kate's parents, unused to speaking publicly about their daughter's romance with the Prince, looked over-awed as photographers, reporters and TV camera crews congregated outside their home. Michael Middleton prepared a statement that he read out: 'I would just like to say that Carole and I are absolutely delighted by today's announcement and thrilled at the prospect of a wedding some time next year. As you know, Catherine and Prince William have been going out together for quite a number of years which has been great for us because we have got to know William very well. We all think he is wonderful and we are extremely fond of him. They make a lovely couple, they are great fun to be with, and we've had a lot of laughs together. We wish them every happiness for the future.'

The Queen said she was 'absolutely delighted' and Prime Minister David Cameron, who had received the news in a call from Buckingham Palace during a cabinet meeting, said it was greeted with 'a great cheer and banging of the table' from fellow ministers.

Prince Harry, who was on flying training in Hampshire, said he was 'delighted' his brother had 'popped the question', adding: 'It means I get a sister which I have always wanted.'

PREVIOUS SPREAD: Rebecca Holmes touches up Catherine's make-up as the royal couple go on display at Madame Tussaud's, April 2012.

LEFT: Catherine's parents announced that they were 'thrilled at the prospect' of their daughter's marriage to Prince William.

The Countess of Wessex said that the Royal Family was 'absolutely thrilled and we all wish them all the luck and love in the world.'

William's uncle, Earl Spencer, the brother of Princess Diana, said in a statement, 'It's wonderful news. Very exciting. My family are all thrilled for them both."

Later that day they gave their first interview together to ITV News' political editor, Tom Bradby, which was broadcast that evening. Seated next to each other on a settee in a room at Clarence House, she wore a dark blue, long-sleeved Issa dress, gathered at the waist, while William wore a dark suit, white shirt and tie.

William recalled the seeds of their romance at university and how they had so much fun together. 'We were friends for over a year first and it just sort of blossomed,' he said. 'We just spent more time with each other, had a good giggle, lots of fun and realised we shared the same interests and had a really good time. She's got a really naughty sense of humour, which kind of helps me because I've got a really dry sense of humour.'

And Kate revealed that she isn't as calm and self-assured as she might appear. Asked what she first thought of William, she looked at him and giggled, 'Well I actually think I went bright red when I met you and sort of scuttled off, feeling very shy.'

She put to bed the rumour that she had a picture of William on her bedroom wall as a young girl, despite William teasing her that 'There wasn't just one. There were about 20.' Instead, she said, she had stuck up a poster of a Levi's model.

In this candid and charming interview William told how he was instantly intrigued about Kate from the very first moment he had met her at university.

'When I first met Kate I knew there was something very special about her and we ended up being good friends for quite a while and that was a good foundation,' he said.

Asked about their split in 2007, William said it was due to them being young and finding their way in life.

'We did split up for a bit,' he said. 'We were both very young, it was at university, we were both finding ourselves as such and being different characters and stuff. It was very much trying to find our own way and we were growing up.'

However Kate, all but confirming that it was William's decision and not hers, was not so insouciant back then. 'I, at the time, wasn't very happy about it,' she admitted, 'but actually it made me

TOP: The press assembled for the official engagement photocall at Buckingham Palace, November 2010.

BOTTOM RIGHT: Catherine denied rumours that she had had posters of William on her bedroom wall when she was growing up, November 2010.

BOTTOM LEFT: The couple examine the ring that meant so much to William, November 2010.

a stronger person. You find out things about yourself that maybe you hadn't realised. I think you can get quite consumed by a relationship when you are younger and I really valued that time for me although I didn't think it at the time.'

As for the long-awaited proposal, William said that it hadn't come as a great surprise to his fiancée because they had been talking about it for a long while. But he knew that he would have to wait until his military training was over before he could focus his attention on his personal life. However, Kate said that she was completely surprised when he did actually propose in Kenya.

'We were out there with friends and I really didn't expect it at all, so it was a total shock and I'm very excited,' she said. Then, with a coy look at her prince she added, 'It was very romantic. There's a true romantic in there.' William nodded, with a sheepish grin.

William revealed that he had been carrying the engagement ring around in his rucksack for 'about three weeks' prior to the proposal and had been terrified he would lose it. 'Everywhere I went I was keeping hold of it because I knew this thing – if it disappeared, I would be in a lot of trouble,' he said. 'I'd been planning it for a while but as every guy out there will know; it takes a certain amount of motivation to get yourself going. And it felt very right in Africa. It was beautiful.'

In a poignant moment he explained why he wanted to give Kate his mother's ring. 'It's my mother's engagement ring so I thought it was quite nice because obviously she's not going to be around to share any of the fun and excitement of it all. This was my way of keeping her close to it all.'

Gazing down at the ring, Kate remarked, 'It's beautiful. I just hope I look after it. It's very, very special.'

William said that they were both relieved that they no longer had to keep their engagement secret. 'We're like ducks – very calm on the surface, with little feet going under the water. It's been really exciting because we've been talking about it for a long time, so for us, it's a real relief and it's really nice to be able to tell everybody.'

His mother's rocky marriage to Prince Charles was also brought to mind when Bradby asked William why he took so long to propose. He answered, 'I wanted to give her a chance to see in, and to back out if she needed to before it all got too much. I'm trying to learn from lessons done in the past and I just wanted to give her the best chance to settle in and to see what happens on the other side.'

The Royal Family might be the very bastion of tradition but William revealed how he went against convention in proposing to Kate before asking permission from her father.

'I was torn between asking Kate's dad first and then the realisation that he might actually say "No" dawned upon me,' he explained. 'So I thought if I ask Kate first, then he can't really say no.'

He added that he had a good relationship with the Middletons. 'Kate's got a very, very close family. I get on really well with them and I'm very lucky that they've been so supportive. Mike and Carole have been really loving and caring and really fun and have been really welcoming towards me, so I've felt really a part of the family.'

As for starting a family of their own, Kate said that she hoped they would be able to have their own 'happy family' at some stage. William added, 'I think we'll take it one step at a time. We'll sort of get over the marriage first and then maybe look at the kids. But obviously we want a family so we'll have to start thinking about that.'

But Kate admitted that she was nervous about what the future held for her as a member of the Royal Family. 'It's obviously nerve-wracking. I don't know the ropes. William is obviously used to it but I'm willing to learn quickly and work hard. I really hope I can make a difference, even in the smallest way. I am looking forward to helping as much as I can.'

William reassuringly tapped her knee with his hand and said, 'She will do very well.'

After the interview the couple posed for photographs at St James's Palace in front of the world's press. In an echo of the pose that Prince Charles and Diana struck 29 years earlier, when he announced their engagement, Kate looped her arm through William's and smiled happily at him.

Amidst a flurry of camera flashes and rapid questions, Kate said, 'It's quite a daunting prospect but hopefully I'll take it in my stride, and William's a great teacher so hopefully he'll be able to help me along the way. I'm really looking forward to spending my time with William.'

Following their engagement interview, copies of Kate's ring and dress were quickly produced to fit all budgets and they all quickly sold out.

On 23 November it was announced that the royal wedding would take place on Friday 29 April 2011 at Westminster Abbey. Disclosing

TOP: Carole, Michael and Pippa Middleton relaxing at the Wimbledon Tennis Championships in the wake of the Royal Wedding, June 2011.

BOTTOM LEFT AND RIGHT: Catherine visiting Leicester Cathedral with the Queen, March 2012.

LEFT: Catherine and William paid a visit to Anglesey, where they were later to set up home together, February 2011.

the news to journalists, the prince's private secretary, Jamie Lowther-Pinkerton, with a mind to the difficult economic climate, stressed that the bulk of the wedding costs would be shared between the two families.

'We know that the world will be watching and the couple are very, very keen indeed that the spectacle should be a classic example of what Britain does best,' he said.

'Prince William and Catherine have made it very clear that they wish everybody to be able to enjoy the day with them. Consequently, the day will be a proper celebration for the nation and the realms.

'Having said that, the couple are very mindful of the current [economic] situation, and for example, Prince William has already expressed a clear wish that any involvement by the armed forces should rely in great part on those servicemen and women already committed to public and ceremonial duties.' He added that, 'The Royal family and the Middleton family will pay for the wedding.'

William had shown his determination for his late mother to play a part in his wedding and this continued when he asked her favourite photographer, Mario Testino, to take the official engagement pictures, which were released on 11 December.

Testino had taken one of the most memorable pictures of Princess Diana at a photo-shoot for *Vanity Fair* one month before she died. The two official engagement pictures were contrasting ones. One was more formal than the other, showing the couple standing in a drawing room at St James's Palace, gently holding each other. She is wearing a white Reiss dress and pearl earrings and William is in a smart grey suit, white shirt and blue tie.

But the second picture is shot in a similar vein to that of Testino's portrait of Princess Diana. It is very informal with the Prince wearing a grey cashmere jumper over an open-necked white shirt and Kate in a cream silk blouse from Whistles. They hug warmly and beam at the camera as the light through the window behind them lends a pleasing softness and warmth to the portrait.

With Kate now a royal fiancée, she was invited, for the first time, to the Queen's annual pre-Christmas lunch at Buckingham Palace, along with royals including Prince Charles, Camilla and Prince Harry.

William and Kate's first public appearance since their engagement was at a charity Christmas variety show on 18 December in aid of the Teenage Cancer Trust at the Thursford Collection in Fakenham, Norfolk.

Just a few days before Christmas came news of a second royal wedding – that of Zara Phillips and Mike Tindall.

William spent Christmas Day at RAF Valley in Anglesey, where he had volunteered for duty; Kate was at her parents' home and the Queen and other members of the Royal Family gathered at Sandringham.

Clarence House made a very modern announcement about further wedding details at the beginning of January 2011 – on the social networking site Twitter. It revealed that Kate would be transported to Westminster Abbey not in the traditional horse-drawn glass carriage, but by car. It was also disclosed that the Archbishop of Canterbury Rowan Williams would marry the couple, the Dean of Westminster the Very Rev Dr John Hall would conduct the 11.00 a.m. service, and the Bishop of London, the Rt Rev Richard Chartres, would give the address.

The couple would then return to Buckingham Palace in a carriage along a route that included Parliament Square, Whitehall, Horse Guards Parade and The Mall before making a traditional balcony appearance at the Palace. After that the Queen would hold a reception for them. This would be followed by a less formal private dinner and dance for close friends and family, hosted by the Prince of Wales.

With an eye to the future and a further attempt to make this a modern union, the Government began discussions about constitutional changes to the Act of Settlement which dictates that sons take precedence over their older sisters in the Royal succession. There was much support for amending this so that daughters would have the same rights as their brothers, meaning that if William and Kate's first-born was a girl, she could become Queen.

In mid-February, more wedding details were disclosed, although they were hardly surprising. Prince Harry was to be best man to his brother and Kate's sister, Pippa, would be her maid of honour. The couple had also asked young relatives and children of their friends' to act as bridesmaids and page boys. They were: Lady Louise Windsor, the seven-year-old daughter of Prince Edward and the Countess of Wessex; the Hon Margarita Armstrong-Jones, eight-year-old daughter of Viscount and Viscountess Linley; Grace van Cutsem, three-year-old daughter of Hugh and Rose van Cutsem; Eliza Lopes, also three, the Duchess of Cornwall's granddaughter; Billy Lowther-Pinkerton, the 10-year-old son of Jamie Lowther-Pinkerton; and eight-year-old Tom

RIGHT: The couple had been invited to launch a new inshore lifeboat in Anglesey, February 2011.

Pettifer, son of William's former nanny, Tiggy Legge-Bourke.

Later that month, Kate and William launched a new RNLI lifeboat in Anglesey. On a blustery day, she wore a three-quarter-length beige herringbone tweed coat with brown trim designed by Katherine Hooker, a chocolate-coloured pashmina and suede ankle boots and a feather fascinator in her wind-swept hair.

After William had made a speech she poured a bottle of champagne over the lifeboat in the traditional launch fashion as William joked, 'She gets to do the fun bit.' Afterwards she happily went around saying hello to the crowd and shaking hands and she burst out laughing when one gentleman gallantly kissed her hand.

The following day they made a nostalgic trip back to St Andrews University to mark its 600th anniversary and a new appeal for funds. But whereas in their student days they had tried to keep out of the glare of publicity, now they were the centre of attention!

There were bagpipes, a military fly-past and a large crowd of well-wishers behind crush-barriers waiting to greet them.

Kate spoke to her former art history tutor, Professor Brendan Cassidy, and told him she had kept all her essays. In a speech to undergraduates wearing their traditional red robes, as well as lecturers, in St Salvator's Quadrangle, William used his fiancée's formal name instead of the usual 'Kate'.

He said, 'This is a special moment for Catherine and me. It feels like coming home.' And he received a loud cheer when he declared St Andrews as 'the best university in the world.'

Kate looked striking in a scarlet fitted jacket with black belt and a matching skirt, teamed with black tights, knee-high boots and gloves.

After leaving St Andrews, the couple flew to the New Zealand High Commission in London where, accompanied by Prince Harry, they signed the book of condolence for victims of the recent New Zealand earthquake. She signed her name as 'Catherine.' It seemed that the couple already had in mind that she would one day be Queen and 'Queen Kate' was, well, not quite right.

The following month they arrived in Belfast for a visit which had been kept top secret because of security fears. Kate showed off her pancake flipping skills on Shrove Tuesday as she expertly wielded a pan at a cancer charity event at Belfast City Hall. And the Prince playfully took on a six-year-old girl and managed to flip his pancake high in the air and caught it in the pan with some aplomb. Kate happily showed off her engagement ring to admiring women in the crowd.

The couple were later special guests at a musical showcase at Youth Action Northern Ireland, where Protestant and Catholic students train together in performing arts. After lunch at Hillsborough Castle, where they met the Northern Ireland Secretary, they spent the afternoon at an agricultural college near Antrim. At the college's florist, Kate was shown a wedding bouquet and helped to make another while William told onlookers that he was leaving the choice of their own wedding-day flowers up to his bride.

'I will let Kate do the chatting about flowers,' he said. 'I am out of my depth.' Kate told one well-wisher, 'I have been to lots of friends' weddings but I never realised how much there was to do.'

Since their engagement the couple had been overwhelmed by the amount of people wanting to give them wedding presents and so they asked instead for donations to be given to a charity fund they had set up supporting 26 various charities.

A statement issued by Clarence House said, 'Having been touched by the goodwill shown them since the announcement of their engagement, Prince William and Miss Middleton have asked that anyone who might wish to give them a wedding gift consider giving instead to a charitable fund. Many of the charities are little known, without existing royal patronage, and undertake excellent work within specific communities. They are charities that have a particular resonance with Prince William and Miss Middleton and reflect issues in which the couple have been particularly interested in their lives to date.'

Clarence House also announced that month that Prince William and his new bride would be driven from Westminster Abbey to Buckingham Palace in the open–topped State landau that carried the Prince and Princess of Wales past cheering crowds after their wedding in 1981. Built in 1902 for King Edward VII's coronation, the landau is pulled by four horses, with two postilions, or riders, on the front pair.

As for the wedding cake, the prestigious honour of creating it when to Leicestershire-based Fiona Cairns, whose cakes are sold in Harrods, Selfridges and the supermarket chain Waitrose.

She was asked to make a traditional multi-tiered fruitcake, decorated with cream and white icing, featuring an English rose, Scottish thistle, Welsh daffodil and Irish shamrock plus the couple's monogram, which would be released on their wedding day.

Kate's wedding ring was made of Welsh gold made by Wartski,

TOP: Catherine flips a pancake on a visit to Belfast with William, March 2011.

BOTTOM: Catherine arriving at the Goring Hotel in London the evening before her wedding, 28 April, 2011.

LEFT: With Pippa by her side, Catherine prepares to spend her last night as a single woman, 28 April 2011.

a family firm that has supplied the monarchy for generations. It was a plain, slim band from a nugget of gold given to Prince William by the Queen shortly after the engagement was announced. Welsh gold has been used for royal brides since the wedding of the Duke of York, later King George VI, to Lady Elizabeth Bowes–Lyon in 1923.

Prince William had chosen not to wear a wedding ring out of 'personal preference' said St James's Palace.

With 17 days to go before her wedding, Kate confessed to a well-wisher that she was feeling increasingly nervous, as she made her final public appearance with William as a single woman. They had arrived in the pouring rain to open Darwen Aldridge Community Academy in Darwen, Lancashire. Later they visited nearby Whitton Country Park in Blackburn, where Kate waved a flag to start a student 100-metre race.

Eight days before the wedding the Queen and Prince Philip finally got to meet Kate's parents when they were invited to a private lunch at Windsor Castle. Although, like Kate, they had been to occasions such as the graduation ceremony at St Andrews and William's passing out parade at Sandhurst, this was the first time that they had properly met and spoken to each other.

Two days before the wedding, Kate drove from her parents' house in Bucklebury, Berkshire, to London with Pippa, to begin her final wedding preparations. She would be staying at Clarence House before joining her family at the Goring Hotel, just around the corner from Buckingham Palace, the night before the wedding.

After dining with Kate at Clarence House, William delighted the crowd lining the Mall outside when he took an impromptu evening stroll, accompanied by Harry, to say hello. He told some well-wishers that he felt nervous and another, 'All I have to do is remember my lines.'

CHAPTER EIGHT

THE ROYAL WEDDING

On the morning of the wedding the Queen bestowed on Prince William the title of Duke of Cambridge, meaning Kate would become HRH the Duchess of Cambridge after their wedding. He also became the Earl of Strathearn and Baron Carrickfergus, and Kate the Countess of Strathearn and Baroness Carrickfergus

The title of Duke of Cambridge dates back to the 17th century when James II, Britain's last Roman Catholic monarch, conferred the title on his four sons. Sady, all of them died in infancy.

Crowds thronged the wedding route – many had slept overnight; others for longer! Those unable to find a space headed to Trafalgar Square where giant screens had been constructed which would relay televised pictures of the wedding proceedings. There was estimated to be up to a million lining the streets of London with two billion following the service on television sets around the world.

Along The Mall, where people of all ages enthusiastically waved Union flags, they started singing patriotic songs such as the National Anthem and Rule Britannia. But there were also some less formal ones such as Get Me To The Church On Time!

Even the band of the Coldstream Guards, resplendent in their scarlet tunics with gold brocade and bearskin hats, got into the spirit of things, marching down the Mall to huge cheers as they played Barry Manilow's Copacabana!

Westminster Abbey is one of the most historically rich and important sites in the country. Benedictine monks first came to the site to worship in the middle of the tenth century. St Edward the Confessor built a new Abbey Church at Westminster in the eleventh century and it has seen the coronation of Kings and Queens since 1066, many of whom are buried here, along with eminent statesmen, soldiers, writers and artists including Geoffrey Chaucer, Charles Dickens, Oliver Cromwell, George Frederic Handel, Rudyard Kipling, David Livingstone and Laurence Olivier. Edward himself was buried here at the heart of the church.

The present Westminster Abbey dates back to 1245 when it was built in the reign of Henry III. With its gothic vaults and arches, marble columns, imposing burial shrines, magnificent stained glass windows, grand altar and long nave it has a theatre-like quality perfect for ceremonial occasions.

The famous landmark had been the burial place for 17 Kings and Queens and the setting for 38 coronations and 15 Royal weddings

PREVIOUS PAGE: The balcony kiss at Buckingham Palace that everyone had been waiting for.

THIS PAGE: Well wishers on The Mall and in Hyde Park, joining in the celebrations. Many camped out overnight to catch a glimpse of the newlyweds.

before William and Kate were married here.

But what would be the happiest day in any groom's life was tainted by William's memories of another Royal gathering here 14 years earlier for the funeral of his mother, Princess Diana. And she was very much in his mind on this very special day.

Guests started to arrive at the Abbey from 8.15 a.m., entering the Great North Door. As well as the British Royal Family and other royals from around the world, plus politicians, ambassadors and diplomats were celebrity friends of William and Kate's and Prince Charles and Camilla. England footballer David Beckham and his former Spice Girl wife Victoria received a big cheer on their arrival, as did Sir Elton John and his partner David Furnish and Rowan Atkinson.

John and Belle Robinson, owners of Jigsaw, in whose Mustique villa William and Kate had stayed, were there as well as several friends from the island including Basil Charles, owner of Basil's Bar. Kate had invited her former headmaster at Marlborough College, Edward Gould, and one of her oldest friends Alicia Fox-Pitt, who had persuaded her to join the Sisterhood charity boat race crew.

Also there was Tom Bradby who had conducted the ITN engagement interview, along with his wife Claudia, a jewellery designer who had worked with Kate at Jigsaw. There were 1,900 guests in all, packed into the Abbey.

The imposing interior had been 'softened' by Kate's desire to have a seasonal flower and nature theme with an emphasis placed on the 'language of flowers'. And so, in the days leading up to the wedding, trees of English field maples and hornbeams were moved in to create a 'living avenue' under which guests would walk to their seats.

The English field maple symbolises humility and reserve, and was used to make loving cups in medieval times, while the hornbeam signifies resilience.

Shane Connolly, the florist chosen to decorate the Abbey and to make the bride's bouquet, said, 'Catherine is a dream client … like few other brides I've ever met. She has an incredibly good eye. Right from the beginning she wanted it to be English, natural, seasonal, ethical.'

Cream and white flowers included rhododendron, euphorbias, beech and wisteria – mostly from Windsor Great Park – and Solomon's Seal, brought from Sandringham, which symbolises confirmation of love.

LEFT: Princess Anne, the groom's aunt, arrives for the ceremony.

TOP RIGHT: Princesses Beatrice and Eugenie, William's cousins, caused a sensation with their unique headgear.

BOTTOM RIGHT: Zara Philips, also William's cousin, arrives at Westminster Abbey with her then fiancé, England rugby player Mike Tindall.

TOP LEFT: Lily-of-the-valley, representing the return of happiness, lies waiting for the newlyweds in their carriage.

BOTTOM LEFT: The groom and best man arriving at the Abbey.

RIGHT: Carole Middleton, mother of the bride, smiling happily for the gathered crowd.

The whole English garden feel was incongruous and bold in such a building but, somehow, it worked and perfectly encapsulated the duality of royal pomp and circumstance with the wedding of a modern young couple very much in love.

Prior to the wedding, Shane Connolly had disclosed, 'One of the things that has been very important to Catherine and to me are the meanings of flowers and the language of flowers. We've tried, especially in the wedding bouquets, which you'll see on the day, we've tried very much to make beautiful stories. The symbolism means a lot to her and also the sourcing has been hugely important.'

At just after 10.00 a.m. William and Harry left Clarence House in a Bentley, arriving at the Abbey eighteen minutes later. A huge cheer went up from the crowd as he emerged from the car resplendent in the bright red dress uniform and blue sash which he wears as Colonel of the Irish Guards, an honour bestowed on him by the Queen in February. The two Princes waved to onlookers and Harry turned to his brother and asked him, 'Are you okay?' before they went inside.

As they walked down the imposing aisle, William smiled and reassured family and friends in the pews that he was at ease. 'I am very calm, very relaxed,' he said. And he even told one female friend, 'You look beautiful.'

Members of foreign royal families started to arrive from Buckingham Palace shortly afterwards, while nearby at the Goring Hotel, the bride's mother, Carole, wearing a sky blue, wool crepe coat over a matching silk dress, left for the Abbey with her son, James, arriving just before 10.30 a.m. They were followed immediately afterward by members of the British Royal Family.

According to protocol, the last to arrive before the bride and bridesmaids, was Prince Charles and the Duchess of Cornwall and, finally, The Queen and the Duke of Edinburgh.

The Queen wore a primrose dress, while Camilla, the Duchess of Cornwall, opted for a champagne silk ensemble by Anna Valentine, who had also designed her wedding dress.

Meanwhile, Kate was just emerging from the Goring Hotel, giving waiting photographers just the merest glimpse of her wedding dress as she ducked into the waiting Rolls-Royce Phantom VI with her father Michael.

Arriving just one minute late for the service, scheduled for 11.00 a.m., she drew great cheers and gasps of admiration for her dress as she stepped onto the red carpet outside the Great West Door.

The elegant bridal gown was a classic design by Sarah Burton of Alexander McQueen. It featured a strapless, Victorian-style satin corset, narrowed at the waist underneath a long-sleeved, sculpted body of Chantilly lace which had been hand-made by the Royal School of Needlework at Hampton Court Palace. The lace followed the Carrickmacross technique, which originated in County Monaghan, Ireland, in the 1820s. The intricate design incorporated rose, thistle, daffodil and shamrock – the emblems of England, Scotland, Wales and Northern Ireland.

The main body of the skirt in ivory and white satin was designed to suggest an opening flower with soft pleats which unfolded to the floor and finished in a 9-foot (2.7-metre) train.

In a statement, Clarence House explained that Kate had 'wished for her dress to combine tradition and modernity with the artistic vision that characterises Alexander McQueen's work,' adding that she chose the brand 'for the beauty of its craftsmanship, respect for traditional workmanship and the technical construction of the clothing.'

Sarah Burton said she wished to give the bride a gown that was 'distinctive, contemporary and feminine.' Her ivory duchesse satin shoes were handmade by the McQueen team.

Kate's diamond Cartier tiara had been lent to her by the Queen for the day. Made in 1936, it was bought by the Duke of York for his wife, the late Queen Elizabeth the Queen Mother, who gave it to her daughter, Queen Elizabeth on her 18th birthday.

Her beautiful earrings were a present from her parents, commissioned from the jewellers, Robinson Pelham. They featured a diamond set acorn suspended in the centre of a pear shape encrusted with diamonds. The design was inspired by the new Middleton coat of arms which features oak leaves and acorns.

She held a simple shield-shaped white bouquet, designed by Shane Connolly, which included seasonal 'English garden' type flowers of lily-of-the-valley, hyacinth, sweet William – perhaps in tribute to her husband – and myrtle.

The 'language of flowers' was once more prominent in the bride's choice of flowers. Lily-of-the-valley represents the return of happiness, sweet William is for gallantry, hyacinth for constancy of love, ivy for fidelity, marriage, wedded love, friendship and affection and myrtle, the emblem of marriage and love.

The inclusion of myrtle is a tradition in the Royal family dating

TOP: According to protocol, the Queen and Prince Philip were the last to arrive before the bride.

BOTTOM: Catherine and her father in their limousine on the way to the Abbey.

TOP: As maid of honour, Pippa was there to greet her sister on her arrival.

BOTTOM: Pippa helps to handle the 9-foot (2.7 metre) train.

back to Queen Victoria. She had planted myrtle against a wall at her home, Osbourne House, on the Isle of White in 1845. When the Queen's daughter, Victoria, married in 1858, a sprig was cut from the plant for her wedding bouquet. And Royal brides have followed this tradition ever since, taking a sprig from the plant at Osbourne House.

After her wedding in 1947, Queen Elizabeth II decided to re-plant the sprig of myrtle from her bridal bouquet to make another bush. Florist Shane Connolly used a sprig from both myrtle bushes for Kate's bouquet.

Following another tradition, Kate's flowers were placed on the grave of the 'Unknown Warrior' in the Abbey after the wedding by a royal officer.

This tradition began in 1923 following the wedding of Lady Elizabeth Bowes-Lyon, the future Queen Elizabeth, to the Duke of York, who later became George VI. She left her bouquet at the grave in memory of her brother Fergus, a young officer who was killed on the Western Front in 1915.

The grave contains the body of an unknown British soldier brought from France to be buried there on 11 November 1920.

As Kate arrived, she was greeted by her sister and maid of honour, Pippa, who had arrived shortly before with the bridesmaids and page boys. She was also in a Sarah Burton dress of ivory and satin crepe with cowl front and cap sleeves. The sisters' parents had given Pippa a pair of floral diamond earrings as a present, designed, like Kate's, by Robinson Pelham. And she wore lily-of-the-valley in her hair, which was styled identically to Kate's in a demi-chignon.

The four young bridesmaids' dresses were handmade by Nicky Macfarlane, the children's wear designer, and her daughter, Charlotte. And the pages wore a uniform in the style of that worn by a Regency foot guards officer, made by Kashket and Partners, which also fitted Prince William's uniform for the wedding.

Michael Middleton held his eldest daughter by the arm as he proudly led her down the aisle. She smiled nervously as she passed the congregation of friends, relatives, dignitaries and celebrities, no doubt a little overawed by the history and majesty of the Abbey and the fairytale reality that she was marrying her Royal Prince.

With TV cameras trained on the wedding party as they made their way down the aisle, it was Pippa Middleton at the rear, holding the 9-foot-long train, who dominated television screens around the world. Tanned, elegant, serene and confident, she won many admirers in her form-fitting dress and social network sites Facebook and Twitter were buzzing with flattering comments.

Meanwhile, William and his best man, Harry, waited at the altar with Dr Rowan Williams, the Archbishop of Canterbury. William stared straight ahead but Harry, with a mischievous grin that he wore all day, looked round then turned back to William to whisper, 'Right, she's here now.'

William looked at her and murmured, 'You look beautiful … just beautiful.' Then, glancing at Michael, he made a joke about the grandness of the occasion. 'Just a small family affair!' he said.

The uplifting vocals of the Westminster Abbey Choir and the Choir of the Chapel Royal filled the Abbey with beautiful and stirring music from the London Chamber Orchestra, the Fanfare Team from the Central Band of the Royal Air Force and the State Trumpeters of the Household Cavalry.

As the marriage vows approached, memories of Princess Diana's famous slip when she repeated the Prince of Wales's Christian names in the wrong order came floating back. But Kate confidently got through them. As expected, she did not promise to 'obey' her husband, but followed the precedent of Princess Diana, who promised only to 'love, comfort, honour and keep' her husband.

Prince William spoke his vows louder than Kate and when he said 'I will' cheers from the crowd outside – listening to the proceedings on loudspeakers – could be heard inside.

But having got their vows over with successfully there was an unexpected hitch and an agonising wait for millions watching on TV at home when the Prince struggled to get the wedding ring onto Kate's finger. For a moment it looked like it just wasn't going to go on but in the end he gave it an extra push which did the trick!

The Archbishop of Canterbury completed the ceremony by joining their right hands together with the words: 'Those whom God hath joined together let no man put asunder.'

The couple wrote their own prayer, which was read by the Right Rev Richard Chartres, Lord Bishop of London, during his sermon. 'God our Father, we thank you for our families; for the love that we share and for the joy of our marriage. In the busyness of each day keep our eyes fixed on what is real and important in life and help us to be generous with our time and love and energy. Strengthened by our union help us to serve and comfort those who suffer. We ask this in the Spirit of Jesus Christ. Amen.'

TOP: Catherine seemed very relaxed as she arrived, taking time to wave to well-wishers.

BOTTOM LEFT: The lacework on Catherine's dress was hand-made at the Royal School of Needlework at Hampton Court Palace.

BOTTOM RIGHT: Like Catherine's dress, Pippa's was designed by Sarah Burton of Alexander McQueen.

TOP: Catherine walked up the aisle flanked by English field maple and hornbeam trees brought in specially to decorate the Abbey.

BOTTOM: At first the ring just wouldn't go on!

The couple were then led to the Chapel of St Edward the Confessor, behind the altar, where they could escape the public glare for a welcome few minutes as they signed the marriage register with their witnesses, the Prince of Wales and Duchess of Cornwall, Prince Harry and Michael, Carole and Pippa.

The Royals emerged from the Chapel to a rapturous fanfare as the newly-weds, grinning widely, walked back down the aisle and out into the sunshine to peals of bells and cheers.

As they stepped into the State Landau which was to take them to Buckingham Palace, they waved to the crowds and even William was overwhelmed. He looked at Kate, seated in the very same seat as Princess Diana had sat after her wedding to Prince Charles, and said, 'Oh my gosh, so many people.'

Prince Harry and Pippa Middleton left the Abbey arm-in-arm with a smiling Harry chatting animatedly. Harry then got into an open carriage behind his brother with bridesmaids Lady Louise Windsor, Eliza Lopes and pageboy Tom Pettifer.

Pippa travelled in another carriage with the three other children, Billy Lowther-Pinkerton, Grace van Cutsem and Margarita Armstrong-Jones.

Along the way Prince Harry encouraged the youngsters seated with him to wave to the crowd.

As William and Kate's carriage drew into the quadrangle of Buckingham Palace, William gallantly helped his bride down the steps.

For the huge crowd gathered in front of the palace waving their union flags — many of whom had camped out for days to get a good view — the highlight of their day was still to come. Prince Charles had rather awkwardly kissed Prince Diana on the balcony at the Palace on their wedding day, after persistent encouragement from the crowd. If William and Kate didn't seal their union with the most public kiss in the world, then there would be widespread disappointment.

Anticipation reached fever point as shadows were seen behind the balcony doors. Then they opened and out stepped the Royal Family. Kate was taken aback by the sea of faces and the loudness of the cheers below her, 'Oh wow!' she said. 'This is amazing.'

Prince Harry, who seemed more excitable than anyone on the day, joked with his grandfather, the Duke of Edinburgh, teasing him that he was smaller than the bride. And the Duke good naturedly laughed.

Soon the crowd was chanting, 'Kiss! Kiss! Kiss!' William looked at Kate and they answered public demand. But as the throng cheered with delight, it was all too much for three-year-old bridesmaid Grace van Cutsem, who grumpily covered her ears with her hands!

But the crowd wanted more and beseeched William to 'kiss her again!' Laughing, he turned to his bride and said, 'Shall we do another kiss? One more? Come on!' And this time it was a more lingering embrace.

Then it was time for the fly-past from the Battle of Britain Memorial Flight – a Lancaster, Spitfire and Hurricane aircraft. Seconds later, four fighter jets flew over in the shape of a diamond.

With a final wave, the gathering on the balcony moved back inside where a wedding breakfast for 650 guests was taking place in the picture gallery.

Claire Jones, the Prince of Wales's official harpist, played as canapes and champagne were handed around to the guests in the elegant Picture Gallery where the magnificent wedding cake attracted much attention.

It had eight tiers and was made from 17 individual fruit cakes, coated in white icing with elaborate iced floral decorations including roses, acorns, and sweet William. A garland design around the fourth tier reflected the architectural designs in the Picture Gallery.

The newly-weds were also sent a cake made by McVities – a chocolate and biscuit creation made from a Royal Family recipe which was specially requested by Prince William.

The reception ended at 3.30 p.m. and William, who had changed into a black frock-coat of the Irish Guards, drove his new bride away from the palace in his father's 1969, open-top, blue Aston Martin Volante, decorated with red, white and blue ribbons and balloons bearing the couple's initials W and C. They headed for Clarence House for a few hours' rest ahead of the evening reception at Buckingham Palace.

Michael, Carole and Pippa Middleton, were greeted with cheers as they arrived back at the Goring Hotel for a private party with relatives and friends.

The black-tie evening reception, hosted by Prince Charles at Buckingham Palace, started at 7.00 p.m., going on until late, with dancing. The Queen and the Duke had decided to absent themselves from this part of the day's schedule. Kate wore her second Sarah Burton outfit of the day, a strapless white satin evening gown with a circle skirt

RIGHT: Prince William and Catherine, now Duchess of Cambridge, Countess of Strathearn and Baroness Carrickfergus, leave the Abbey as husband and wife.

and diamanté embroidered detail around the waist.

She and William left Clarence House for Buckingham Palace shortly after 8.00 p.m. in a Jaguar with tinted windows. About half an hour earlier, the Middletons and some guests had clambered into a minibus for the short journey from the Goring to the Palace. Pippa had changed into a long emerald green sleeveless dress with a jewelled embellishment and a plunging neckline, while Carole wore a black, capped sleeve dress with a tiered skirt.

Singer Ellie Goulding, best known for her version of Elton John's 'Your Song', was among those performing at the event as guests relaxed and let their hair down now that the formal and traditional part of the day was over.

Their honeymoon was delayed for a while as William went back to work four days after the wedding – and his first day back proved to be a particularly dramatic one. Meanwhile, Kate was coming to terms with life as a royal wife and the heady thought that she might one day be Queen!

PREVIOUS SPREAD: Having arrived in motorised transport, pageantry went into full swing when the bride, groom and wedding party travelled by horse-drawn carriage from the Abbey to Buckingham Palace.

BOTTOM: Catherine's reaction when she saw the crowds was, 'Oh my gosh, so many people.'

TOP RIGHT: What the people had come to see …

BOTTOM RIGHT: Prince William borrowed his father's Aston Martin for the trip from Buckingham Palace to St James Palace.

CHAPTER NINE

MARRIED INTO 'THE FIRM'

Having returned to Anglesey after their fairytale wedding, Kate said goodbye to her new husband as he went off to work – much like any average married couple!

But Kate was a royal and a Forces wife and both have their own demands. Their honeymoon was delayed because William did not get any preferential treatment from the search and rescue team and any further holiday break would need to be split up to fit around shifts.

William's first day back at work was a busy one. He was involved in two emergencies. In the first, his Sea King helicopter was sent to rescue a 70-year-old man who suffered a heart attack while on Lliwedd, a mountain in Snowdonia National Park, and was airlifted to hospital. Soon after, William and his three fellow crew members had to pick up four off-duty policemen who were stuck on Snowdon because one of them suffered vertigo as they made their way down from the peak.

Ten days after their wedding the royal couple flew out on a private jet to the Seychelles on their honeymoon. They had first visited the islands in August 2007 when they stayed on Desroches. It had been one of their favourite ever holidays.

After landing at the main airport, they were transferred by helicopter to the private North Island where they spent 10 days at a secluded villa with its own butler and stunning view of the turquoise waters of the Indian Ocean. North Island is known for its conservation initiatives – which appealed to William – providing a sanctuary where endangered Seychelles fauna and flora has been re-introduced and given the chance to regenerate.

William and Kate were seen strolling, hand-in-hand, along the appropriately named, Honeymoon Beach, swimming in the balmy waters and sunbathing on a yacht. They enjoyed the wildlife and went on several dives to study the coral reef. An environmental guide also showed them a turtle nest with hatching eggs.

After returning home from this paradise island they had six weeks before flying to Canada on a ten-day tour taking in Ottawa, Alberta, the Northwest Territories, Prince Edward Island and Quebec.

Meanwhile, Prince Charles, who had flown to Washington for an official visit that included a meeting with President Obama, joked with students at Georgetown University that he was pleased he was not making a wedding toast. 'This makes a change from making embarrassing speeches about my eldest son during wedding receptions.'

PREVIOUS SPREAD: William and Catherine at the Calgary Stampede in Canada, July 2011.

TOP LEFT: Catherine's maple leaf hat and the maple leaf brooch lent to her by the Queen for the Royal Tour of Canada, July 2011.

BOTTOM LEFT: Catherine at the morning service aboard HMCS *Montreal* in Champlain Harbour, July 2011.

RIGHT: Meeting street hockey players in Yellowknife, July 2011.

As well as the many royal visits and duties that would be expected of her, Kate also knew that she and William would need to turn their thoughts to starting a family. This too was a 'duty' to provide a royal heir. And at 29, she would not be expected to delay too long. But there were also the more mundane, day-to-day chores to do. She may have walked down the majestic aisle of Westminster Abbey as a royal bride, but in Anglesey she was also regularly spotted walking down the aisle of her local supermarket dressed in a casual top and jeans. She looked just like a regular housewife … but not quite. Because trying not to attract too much attention were her three royal protection officers, trailing as discreetly as they could behind her.

On 11 June, Kate proudly watched William take part in the Trooping of the Colour, the annual parade to mark the Queen's official birthday. The ceremony originated from traditional preparations for battle when regimental 'colours', or flags, were trooped down the ranks so that they could be seen and recognised by the soldiers when they would be in the heat and confusion of battle.

Kate had travelled from Buckingham Palace to Horse Guards Parade in a carriage with Prince Harry, the Duchess of Cornwall and Prince Andrew, and had waved to cheering crowds lining The Mall.

Kate, wearing an ivory, double-breasted, fitted jacket and skirt with a black hat, sat next to Camilla and both shared a tartan quilt pulled over their knees.

Prince William rode a grey charger and wore the same scarlet tunic as he had worn for his wedding but this time with a bearskin hat, in his role as Colonel of the Irish Guards. Riding with him was the Prince of Wales, Colonel of the Welsh Guards, Princess Royal, Colonel of the Household Cavalry's Blues and Royals and the Duke of Kent, Colonel of the Scots Guards.

The Queen arrived in an Ivory Mounted Phaeton with Prince Philip, who celebrated his 90th birthday the day before and was dressed in uniform as Colonel of the Grenadier Guards.

The Queen, whose actual birthday had been on 21 April when she turned 85, inspected the line of troops resplendent in their famous scarlet tunics and bearskins. Four of the five Foot Guards regiments of the Household Division took part – the Welsh, Grenadier, Scots and Coldstream Guards.

Dressed in a pale blue coat and matching hat, she stood with the Duke as the ceremonial flag was paraded past her and the Massed Bands played.

RIGHT: William and Catherine arrive at the Royal Albert Hall for the Our Greatest Team Olympic event, May 2012.

TOP: Pippa with her brother, father and friends during the Thames Pageant Diamond Jubliee celebrations, June 2012.

BOTTOM: Catherine in a cowboy hat enjoying the rodeo in Calgary, July 2011.

Later she joined other members of the Royal Family, including William and Kate on the balcony as the celebration ended with the traditional fly-past of more than 20 aircraft with the Red Arrows display team providing the spectacular finale, flying overhead trailing red, white and blue smoke.

Later that day, Kate joined guests at the wedding of close friend Sam Waley-Cohen, who married party organiser Bella Balin. The dress she wore was an old one that she had been seen in four years earlier when she and Pippa had an evening at Boujis nightclub. It had a bold black and white circle pattern and she teamed it with the same black hat she had worn earlier in the day at The Trooping of the Colour. The two sisters happily chatted with friends when they arrived at St Michael and All Angels Church in Lambourn, near Hungerford in Berkshire, before making their way inside.

At the start of July, Kate and William began their nine-day tour of Canada where they would visit seven cities before heading to the United States. It was their first official tour as a married couple and a memorable one.

In Ottawa they laid flowers at the National War Memorial in Confederation Square and then split up to greet some 3,000 well-wishers some of whom had been calling, 'We love you Kate.' Later they were officially welcomed by Canada's governor general, David Johnston, before a large crowd at Government House. Prime Minister Stephen Harper spoke after the governor general, saying, 'Your journey across our fair dominion marks the beginning of your journey into the hearts of Canadians. We wish you all the best on both counts. We are both honoured and delighted that you have chosen us for your first official tour together.'

And in his speech – delivered partly in French – William replied, 'Catherine and I are so delighted to be here in Canada. Instilled in us by our parents and grandparents, who love this country, we have been looking forward to this moment for a very long time, and before we were married, we both had a longing to come here together. The geography of Canada is unsurpassed and is famous for being matched only by the hospitality of its people.'

In the evening they attended a barbecue, hosted by Mr Johnston, for which Kate wore an old favourite outfit – an Issa bird print wrap dress she wore the day before she got married.

The royal visit was timed to coincide with Canada Day. They arrived at Parliament Hill in an open-topped landau, accompanied by Mounties on horseback amidst sweltering heat, where they took part in a citizenship ceremony. Kate wore the white Reiss dress that she had worn for her official engagement photograph, together with a glittering diamond maple leaf brooch – the national emblem of Canada - which the Queen had loaned her for the tour and a jaunty red hat with a red maple leaf.

The royal couple watched while 25 young men and women became fully-fledged Canadians. Each took the Oath of Citizenship, professing loyalty to the prince's grandmother, the Queen. William then presented them with a folded Canadian flag before Kate handed over a small hand flag.

For the evening celebrations Kate changed into a purple Issa Jersey dress as they watched a two-hour show of variety acts including music and military displays.

The following day they visited a cookery school in Montreal where she was shown how to make a paté starter in apple cider jelly by one of the students. An impressed Kate told her that she liked to cook at home but 'I don't do fancy things.'

Later in the tour they enjoyed the scenery as they hiked through Banff National Park and then visited families whose homes were destroyed in recent forest fires. William and Kate spent a romantic night in a log cabin in Skoki Lodge near Lake Louise in Alberta. They also paddled in a canoe to an island near Yellowknife, Northwest Territories, to watch the dramatic sunset.

After taking part in a street hockey game called 'shinny' in Yellowknife they were presented with hockey jerseys emblazoned with the name 'Cambridge' on the back. Whilst Kate's was numbered '1', William, to their amusement had '2' on his!

At the Calgary Stampede, an annual rodeo and festival, they got into the spirit of things. Both wore white Stetsons and jeans – Kate combining hers with a casual white shirt and William a plaid one. There was a huge cheer after they hit a giant red button to launch fireworks and a cascade of ticker tape marking the start of the annual event which styles itself as 'the greatest outdoor show on earth.'

In his last major speech of the royal trip, the Prince described how Canada had 'far surpassed' what he had been promised and vowed to return.

'In 1939, my great grandmother, Queen Elizabeth the Queen Mother, said of her first tour of Canada with her husband, King George VI, "Canada made us." Catherine and I now know very well

TOP: William and Catherine join in a 'Mexican wave' while watching Any Murray playing at Wimbledon during the Olympic Games, August 2012.

BOTTOM: Watching the Paralympic cycling in the velodrome, August 2012.

what she meant. Canada has far surpassed all that we were promised.
Our promise to Canada is that we shall return.'

Then it was on to a whistle-stop tour of California. The
evening after their plane landed at Los Angeles, they attended a
business event at the Beverly Hilton Hotel supporting UK trade and
investment. There was near hysterical screaming from the crowds
outside as they arrived. Kate wore a lavender Peridot dress by
Serbian-born designer Roksanda Illinic.

Later they moved on to a reception hosted by British Consul-
General Dame Barbara Hay at her Hancock Park residence, where
they would be staying for their visit. Here they were joined by 200
guests for drinks and canapés in the garden, including David Beckham
and Stephen Fry.

Kate wore an emerald green, silk-belted Maja dress by Diane von
Furstenberg, accessorised with beige platform stilettos and a leopard
print clutch bag.

The following day William played in a charity polo match at the
Santa Barbara Polo Club in which he scored four goals. After the
match he kissed Kate on both cheeks to the delight of spectators as
she gave out prizes. Kate, who is allergic to horses, told Clarisa Ru,
the wife of the club's president, she was making good progress. 'I'm
actually allergic to horses, but the more time one spends with them
the less allergic you become,' she said.

In the evening, they mixed with Hollywood 'royalty' such as
Tom Hanks, Nicole Kidman, Quentin Tarantino and Barbra Streisand
at a BAFTA black-tie dinner in Los Angeles celebrating new British
film talent. A crowd of 2,000 screamed as the royal couple arrived
at the Belasco Theater. Kate wore a clinging lilac ballgown by
Alexander McQueen.

Following all this glitz and glamour, they spent their final day
involved with philanthropic work, starting with an event to support
Tusk Trust that raises funds for African wildlife, of which the Prince
is a patron. They also visited Inner-City Arts, an LA program that
provides help through art for disadvantaged and homeless children in
some of the city's most deprived neighbourhoods.

Back home in the UK after their successful tour of North
America and there was another royal wedding approaching. William's
cousin Zara Phillips wed Mike Tindall in a low-key, by British royal
standards, event on 30 July.

All the main Royal Family from the Queen downwards attended

the ceremony at Edinburgh's Canongate Kirk, followed by a reception at the Palace of Holyroodhouse, the Queen's official residence in Scotland, located at the bottom of Edinburgh's famous Royal Mile, at the opposite end to the imposing Edinburgh Castle.

Kate once more showed that she had no intention of being a 'clothes horse' that is only seen draped in the newest designs. Instead she wore a pale gold embroidered coat she last wore in 2006 at the wedding of Laura Parker Bowles.

The previous day, at a pre-wedding cocktail party, she again rummaged around in her wardrobe and found the green Diane von Furstenberg dress she had worn during her tour of Los Angeles.

Kate's wedding dress was displayed at Buckingham Palace during the summer for the public to get a close look at it and it was a hugely popular attraction. Also on display were her shoes, diamond earrings and a replica of her bridal bouquet.

The royal visits continued and at the beginning of November William and Kate visited a UNICEF famine relief depot in Copenhagen. They were greeted by the Crown Prince and Princess of Denmark who walked around the depot with them. All had to wear blue safety helmets. William and Kate were given a taste of a special high-protein peanut paste which was being sent to malnourished children in East Africa. Afterwards they were taken to the airport where they toured a British Airways Boeing 747 which was taking the food and medical supplies to Africa.

But away from the many official visits Kate also found time to attend small charitable concerns that interested her. One of these was a surprise visit to a primary school in Islington, North London, to an art therapy charity.

The school had written to her asking for her support and she went along to find out more about The Art Room charity, based in Oxford, that works with challenging children. The charity has a branch at the school in Islington and staff, pupils and parents there were startled when Kate turned up, at short notice, in casual jeans and a jumper.

The charity pledges to 'increase self-esteem, self-confidence and independence through art' and works with children aged from five to 16 who are disruptive or withdrawn or have learning difficulties. Kate was so impressed that in January 2012 she became patron of The Art Room.

At the start of December, William and Kate, along with

RIGHT: William and Catherine attended a BAFTA event at the Bellasco Theatre while they were in Los Angeles, July 2011.

TOP LEFT: During her Far East tour with William, Catherine attends a state dinner given by the President of Singapore, September 2012.

TOP RIGHT: Arriving for a fund raising event at the Imperial War Museum, London, April 2012.

BOTTOM: Catherine checks her mother-in-law's security pass at the Olympic cross country event, July 2012.

Prince Charles and Camilla as well as Camilla's daughter Laura and daughter-in-law Sara, attended a charity concert at the Royal Albert Hall in London, organised by Take That singer Gary Barlow. Kate combined a short black and cream dress from High Street chain Zara with a black Ralph Lauren jacket.

That Christmas was the first time that Kate, now a member of the Royal Family, spent the festive period at Sandringham. And it turned out to be a dramatic one. After Prince Philip had complained of chest pains, he was airlifted by helicopter to Papworth Hospital, near Cambridge, where surgeons fitted a stent, an artificial tube, to combat a blocked coronary artery. He remained in hospital for four days for observation before being released.

Shortly before Christmas, Kate had been given a black cocker-spaniel puppy from a litter of her parent's dog, Ella. Kate named her Lupo and was to enjoy many walks in the park with her.

The New Year saw a very wet UK premiere of Steven Spielberg's movie adaptation of Michael Morpurgo's First World War novel *War Horse* in London, which was in aid of The Foundation of Prince William and Prince Harry. As they stepped out of their car, a gallant Prince William held an umbrella over his wife, who wore a floor-length black lace and cream Alice Temperley gown, shielding her from the rain.

Director Steven Spielberg spoke about the couple's gesture in attending the event, saying: 'It's a very prestigious honour because they represent an entirely new era in British royalty that has the entire world excited. When they came to America, that was one of the most exciting events, I think, that we've enjoyed for some time, so it's such an honour to be here in the UK to be able to meet them and to be able to show them, and all of us, *War Horse*.'

Six hundred serving and former military personnel and their families also attended the premiere, alongside beneficiaries of military charities with which the Foundation of Prince William and Prince Harry had been working. Thirty donors paid £10,000 to attend which enabled them to mingle with the royals and film stars at the after-show party in the Queen's Gallery of Buckingham Palace.

William's job took him away from Britain when he spent six weeks working in the Falkland Islands. On his return, he joined Kate and her family on a skiing holiday in the French Alps in April.

That summer's Olympics were held in London where the Queen made a memorable appearance in a film screened at the opening ceremony which saw her at Buckingham Palace awaiting James Bond (actor Daniel Craig). The pair are then shown walking out to the lawn and stepping into a waiting helicopter.

RIGHT: Happy memories from the Olympics, summer 2012.

It flies over London to the Olympic Stadium where Bond and a stunt double portraying the Queen, jump out. Their union flag parachutes open as the familiar 007 music kicks in. A few moments later and the Queen and the Duke of Edinburgh arrive for real and make their way to the Royal Box.

It was the first time that the Queen had ever indulged in something so uniquely fun and entertaining and it put a smile on everyone's faces, setting the tone for a remarkably successful games that were organised with expertise combined with a quirky light touch that emanated a charm never seen before.

Kate was a keen attendee at the games. She particularly enjoyed watching the hockey and enthusiastically cheered on the British gymnasts and boxers. William joined her to watch the cycling, along with Prince Harry, and they stood with the rest of the crowd, arms raised in triumph as they cheered British success. Kate also greatly enjoyed the successful Paralympic Games which were to follow.

It was a wonderful summer of sport in Britain and tennis-loving Kate and sister Pippa had cheered and groaned along with other enthralled spectators watching Andy Murray losing to Roger Federer in the final at Wimbledon.

A nine-day visit to South Asia to represent the Queen in her Diamond Jubilee year was a colourful occasion. It began in Singapore mid-September where the couple were shown around a botanical garden. There was a poignant moment when William fought back his emotion when he was shown a white orchid that had been named after his mother. She had died in the Paris car crash just two weeks before she was due to fly out to see it. The Prince said that it was 'beautiful.' They were also honoured to be shown a white orchid named after them.

During their visit to Singapore they laid a wreath at a memorial for Commonwealth casualties from the Second World War, on behalf of the Queen and the Duke of Edinburgh. Moving on to Malaysia, Kate was touched by the work done at a hospice in Kuala Lumpur for terminally ill children. In a speech to staff and patients she called it 'life changing.'

But whilst on their Far East tour a storm was erupting back home when a French magazine named *Closer* – owned by an Italian publisher – published revealing paparazzi pictures of Kate sunbathing topless on the terrace of a chateau in Provence owned by Viscount Linley where they

LEFT: William and Catherine at the National Botanical Gardens during their Singapore visit, September 2012.

BOTTOM: William and Catherine are carried in ornate chairs on arrival in the Solomon Islands, September, 2012.

had been staying earlier in the month for a brief, three-day break. The images were later published by another of the same company's magazines and also by the *Irish Daily Star*.

The Duke and Duchess of Cambridge put on a brave face as they carried on with their official duties during a trip to Borneo. On a trek through a tropical jungle they were swept off their feet when they were hoisted 103 feet (31 metres) into the air on pulleys to enjoy sweeping views above the tree tops. In the Solomon Islands, Kate was given a loose fitting pink bandeau dress to wear and William a blue and white swirly patterned short sleeved cotton shirt.

A delighted Kate became an island princess when she was crowned with a headdress of flowers by activists working to improve the status of women in the Solomon Islands. And William gamely accepted when he was challenged by a 13-year-old goalkeeper to take penalty shots against him. He failed to score!

Their final stop was to Tuvalu where they looked a little bemused to be carried from their plane to the airport terminal on a thatched podium, seated in ornate chairs lifted by 25 men in leaf skirts, accompanied by group of 40 singing women wearing purple dresses covered in cream flowers.

It was the start of a fun visit in which they enjoyed the moment and let their hair down. At a gathering of island communities taking part in a dance contest, Kate was given a colourful skirt to wear and she didn't need much encouragement to get to her feet and follow the traditional dance moves. William was a little more reluctant but eventually he too wore a skirt and showed off his moves.

At the end of their stay they were once more carried back to their plane and flew off with huge smiles on their faces and memories that would live with them forever.

In November they made their first visit to their namesake city, Cambridge, to open a hospital. During a walkabout, William laughed when he was handed a baby outfit by a well-wisher. She had made it especially for him and had embroidered the words 'Daddy's little co-pilot' on the front. The smiling Prince said, 'I'll keep that.'

Kate made a joyous return to the school that she had so adored as a pupil, St Andrew's in Pangbourne, Berkshire, to open a new artificial sports pitch and she couldn't wait to take part in a hockey training session with the team of 12-year-olds. The visit was, appropriately, on St Andrew's Day and she gamely showed off some of her old hockey skills, despite being hindered in an Alexander McQueen tartan frockcoat and knee-high boots with three-inch heels.

Kate, who had spent nine years at the school, told staff and pupils, 'It is such a treat to be back here at St Andrew's. I absolutely loved my time here. They were some of my happiest years which makes it so incredibly exciting to be back here today. In fact, I enjoyed it so much that when I had to leave I told my mother I was going to come back as a teacher. While that didn't quite happen, I was thrilled to have been asked back to join you today on St Andrew's Day.'

Kate had captained the hockey team during her time here as a pupil and told how the school had fired her interest in sporting activities.

'It was while I was here that I realised my love of sport,' she said. 'It has been a huge part of my life and I feel incredibly grateful for the opportunities I had to get outside and play in such wonderful open spaces, though sadly there was nothing quite as glamorous as this [the new pitch] in my time! I hope that you all enjoy playing sport here as much as I used to, and make the most of these incredible facilities.'

Kate had looked fresh faced and radiant during her energetic visit. But just days later she was feeling a little sick …

TOP: William and Catherine remove their shoes before entering a mosque in Kuala Lumpur, Malaysia, September 2012.

BOTTOM LEFT: Catherine covers her head before entering the Assyakirin Mosque in Kuala Lumpur, September 2012.

BOTTOM RIGHT: Catherine receives a posy from Jessica Harris while visiting Victoria Barracks, Windsor, to present medals to the Irish Guards, June 2011.

CHAPTER TEN

A ROYAL HEIR

He sudden news that the Duchess of Cambridge was expecting a baby came unexpectedly and in a highly unusual way, considering how carefully such royal news is normally managed.

She had conceived in October, shortly after returning home from her Far East trip but, because her pregnancy was at such an early stage, she and William had been planning on keeping it a secret for longer. However, after William drove her to hospital just after lunch with a severe form of morning sickness on 3 December 2012 and they were told that Kate would be kept in for the next few days, the couple felt compelled to release a statement.

Kate had been staying with her parents in Berkshire after her visit to her former preparatory school, St Andrew's, just a few minutes' drive away. William had spent the first part of the weekend with friends at a shooting party. When he finally met up with his wife, he became increasingly concerned that she was unable to keep down any food or water. After consulting their doctor, he declined the offer of an ambulance and instead drove her in their Range Rover to the King Edward VII Hospital in London.

A statement from St James's Palace said: 'Their Royal Highnesses the Duke and Duchess of Cambridge are very pleased to announce that the Duchess of Cambridge is expecting a baby. The Queen, the Duke of Edinburgh, the Prince of Wales, the Duchess of Cornwall and Prince Harry and members of both families are delighted with the news.'

It went on to say that the Duchess was suffering from hyperemesis gravidarum, which requires supplementary hydration and nutrients.

'As the pregnancy is in its very early stages, Her Royal Highness is expected to stay in hospital for several days and will require a period of rest thereafter,' it added.

The world's media set up camp outside the hospital but St James's Palace refused to be drawn on when the royal couple became aware of the pregnancy, commenting only that it was 'recently.'

Kate was put on a drip to restore lost nutrients and later given anti-sickness tablets. After a second day in hospital, the Palace said that the Duchess was 'feeling better' and that the couple were 'immensely grateful for the good wishes they have received.'

Prince William, who had arrived earlier that day hunched over and looking tense, dressed in a casual grey jumper, jeans and trainers, was palpably more at ease and even smiled when he left the hospital.

PREVIOUS SPREAD: Catherine and the Queen enjoying a children's sports day in Nottingham during the Queen's Jubilee Tour, June 2012.

TOP LEFT: William outside the King Edward VII Hospital in London visiting Catherine, December 2012.

TOP RIGHT: A worried Carole Middleton heads home after seeing her daughter in hospital, December 2012.

BOTTOM: William and Catherine leaving the hospital, December 2012.

Despite her sickness, the pregnancy marked a day of joy for the nation. Members of the Royal Family, including the Queen and grandfather-to-be Prince Charles, had been informed less than an hour before the statement was issued. Kate's parents had become aware of her condition at the weekend after she had been sick.

Following tradition for Royal mothers-to-be, Kate was looked after by the Queen's gynaecologist, a post currently held by Alan Farthing, who had become widely known to the public as the former fiancé of murdered British TV host Jill Dando. He was quickly on the scene, as was the Queen's former gynaecologist Marcus Setchell, who had delivered both the Earl and Countess of Wessex's children.

The baby, due in mid-July, would be Prince Charles's first grandchild and the Queen's third great-grandchild.

Meanwhile, it was disclosed that the Government had received final consent from all the Commonwealth realms to press ahead with legislation ending discrimination against women in the line of succession to the British throne. Deputy Prime Minister Nick Clegg said that ministers would now introduce the Succession to the Crown Bill in the House of Commons at the 'earliest opportunity' available in the parliamentary timetable.

The legislation would end the principle of male primogeniture, so that the first child of the Duke and Duchess of Cambridge would succeed to the throne, regardless of whether the baby is a girl or a boy.

'This is a historic moment for our country and our monarchy. People across the realms of the Commonwealth will be celebrating the news that the Duke and Duchess of Cambridge are expecting their first child,' Mr Clegg said. 'We can also all celebrate that whether the baby is a boy or a girl, they will have an equal claim to the throne. It's a wonderful coincidence that the final confirmation from the other realms arrived on the very day that the Duke and Duchess of Cambridge made their announcement.'

Meanwhile, bets were being taken on the names of William and Kate's child. Elizabeth was an early favourite for a girl and George for a boy. Other popular bets were Victoria, Diana, Francis and Henry, John and Philip.

But the upbeat mood was shortly to take a sudden downbeat turn when a nurse at the hospital was duped by two radio DJs from Sydney, Australia. The pair made a prank phone call in which they impersonated the Queen and Prince of Wales enquiring about the

TOP: Three-year-old Isobelle Laursen presents Catherine with some flowers during a visit to Humberside Fire and Rescue Service in Grimsby, March 2013.

BOTTOM: Catherine chats with residents from a hospice in Grimsby, March 2013.

Duchess's health. The call was made by Mel Greig and Michael Christian, from a radio station called 2Day FM. They called the hospital in the early hours of the morning and managed to persuade a nurse answering the phone to put them through to the nurse who was keeping watch on Kate.

The duty nurse told them, 'She's sleeping at the moment and has had an uneventful night. She's been given some fluids and she's stable. She hasn't had any retching with me and she's been sleeping on and off.'

The nurse also talked about Prince William's visit. When asked what time he had gone home, she replied 'At about nine o'clock last night.'

Once the hoax was revealed the hospital publicly deplored it but St James's Palace declined to comment.

The DJs later told reporters, 'We were very surprised that our call was put through. We thought we'd be hung up on as soon as they heard our terrible accents. We're very sorry if we've caused any issues and we're glad to hear that Kate is doing well.'

With the row growing, a spokesman for the radio station apologised and stressed the hoax had a humorous, rather than malicious, motive.

Meanwhile, William arrived at the hospital to visit his wife again and spent six hours by her bedside. He was joined by Pippa and James Middleton for an hour in the afternoon. Also visiting in the evening was Carole Middleton.

After three days in hospital, Kate left on 6 December, saying she was feeling 'much better,' and was driven away with a smiling William.

St James's Palace said in a statement: 'The Duchess of Cambridge has been discharged from the King Edward VII Hospital and will now head to Kensington Palace for a period of rest. Their Royal Highnesses would like to thank the staff at the hospital for the care and treatment The Duchess has received.'

Later that day Prince Charles said that he was 'thrilled' that she was pregnant. Appearing at an event aboard HMS Belfast in central London, he added, 'It's a very nice thought to become a grandfather in my old age. I'm very glad my daughter-in-law is getting better, thank goodness.' And he made light of the radio hoax, joking to reporters who had asked how he felt about Kate's pregnancy, 'How do you know I'm not a radio station?'

But the aftermath of the hoax was to have tragic and unexpected consequences when the nurse who had first answered the call and put it through to the duty nurse, committed suicide days later. John Lofthouse, the hospital's chief executive, said, 'Our thoughts and deepest sympathies at this time are with her family and friends. Everyone is shocked by the loss of a much-loved and valued colleague.'

A few hours later the radio station and the company that owns it said that the presenters had been taken off air until further notice, as a mark of respect. The radio presenters were shocked and grief stricken by what had happened.

Michael Christian said he was, 'gutted, shattered, heartbroken.' He added. 'It was something that was just fun and light-hearted and a tragic turn of events no one could have predicted or expected. Our deepest sympathy goes to the family, friends and all those people affected.'

A tearful and pale Mel Greig said, 'Not a minute goes by that we don't think about the family [of the nurse] and what they are going through, and the thought we may have played a part is gut-wrenching. I hope they are okay, I really do.'

Kate had cancelled her immediate engagements and William was to attend the annual British Military Tournament at Earl's Court, West London, without her. But when she had a return of the acute morning sickness, he decided not to go. Instead he remained by his wife's side.

A St James's Palace spokesman said, 'It is well known that hyperemesis gravidarum often recurs.'

At a charity tennis match the previous day, a puzzled William told a guest, 'I don't know why they call it morning sickness – they should call it all-day and all-night sickness.'

A few days later William went to the premiere of *The Hobbit* film in Leicester Square, central London, where his wife received a round of applause in her absence after actor Sir Ian McKellen asked the Prince to pass on everyone's good wishes to her as she recovers.

A touched William replied, 'She would have loved to have been here if she could.'

But Kate rallied to make a welcome TV appearance when she presented the winning trophy at the BBC's annual *Sports Personality of the Year* on 16 December, while William returned to work. She had been a keen supporter of the British Olympic team and enjoyed the opportunity to meet many of the athletes there. The award went

THIS PAGE: Catherine
with William and Prince
Harry on a tour of the new
Warner Bros Studios in
Hertfordshire, April 2013.

to cyclist Bradley Wiggins who had been victorious in the gruelling Tour de France before taking Olympic gold nine days later.

Kate looked well, if a little pale, in an elegant, floor-length, bottle green Alexander McQueen dress. She also presented former athlete and the organiser of the London Olympic Games, Lord Sebastian Coe, with a lifetime achievement award.

Because of her illness, Kate wanted to relax and be in the sanctuary of her family home that Christmas so, instead of joining the other Royals at Sandringham, William spent the festive occasion with the Middletons at their Berkshire home. But Kate did join the Royal Family for their annual pre-Christmas lunch at Buckingham Palace.

At the end of December, the Queen declared that if the Duke and Duchess of Cambridge have a daughter she will be titled Princess rather than Lady. Using Letters Patent, a method by which the Sovereign can give orders without the involvement of Parliament, the Queen decided that from now on 'all the children of the eldest son of the Prince of Wales' should be given the title of Royal Highness 'with the titular dignity of Prince or Princess prefixed to their Christian names.'

Up until then, only the eldest son of the eldest son of the Prince of Wales was entitled to the honour, following a decree made by George V in 1917. This meant that a daughter of William and Kate would have been known as 'Lady.'

As the New Year approached, William was at a crossroads. With Kate expecting their first child in the summer, would he remain in the RAF or finally devote himself to royal duties? He enjoyed being a pilot and also living in Anglesey but work was currently underway in refurbishing a new 20-room apartment at Kensington Palace which would be turned into an impressive family home for him and Kate and their child.

The first official portrait of Kate caused much controversy when it was unveiled in January 2013 at the National Portrait Gallery in central London. It showed Kate, who had recently turned 31, with slightly greying hair, facial lines, the suggestion of bags under her eyes and a rather bulbous nose.

Kate described the oil painting by Paul Emsley as 'amazing' and 'brilliant' and William said it was 'absolutely beautiful', although art critics, in general, were not so enthusiastic.

At the start of February, William and Kate flew out to Mustique for a holiday with her family. The royal couple hired a villa while the Middletons rented a property nearby. But there was to be further paparazzi scandal when an Italian magazine published a photograph of her in a bikini, while walking with William on the beach. It was the same publication that had also published pictures of her in Provence back in September.

Shortly after returning to the UK from the luxury of Mustique, Kate visited an addiction centre in South West London where she spoke to women recovering from substance dependence. In an art therapy class Kate, who at times stood with her hands protectively cupped underneath her stomach, was asked by a recovering alcoholic if she was nervous about having a child. She smiled and replied that it 'would be unnatural if I wasn't.'

On her return from a wedding in the Swiss Alps, Kate visited the sea port of Grimsby in Lincolnshire where a stammered comment caused much speculation that she had inadvertently let slip the sex of her unborn child. Visiting the town's National Fishing Heritage Centre, a woman presented her with a teddy bear to which she replied, 'Thank you, I will take that for my d . . .' then she stopped and said, 'for my baby.' As she moved on, another woman teasingly said, 'You were going to say daughter, weren't you?' Kate replied, 'What do you mean? We, we don't know yet..' But the woman, not willing to give up, said, 'Oh I think you do.' A flustered Kate replied, 'We're not telling.'

A fascinating and humorous insight into the Royal couple's private life was aired in a TV documentary about the monarch, called *Our Queen*. It showed that, just like many married couples, a competitive nature could cause frustration when it came to playing board games!

In the programme, Olympic boxer Anthony Ogogo recounted a conversation with Kate at a Buckingham Palace reception for athletes.

'The Duchess of Cambridge said she was really competitive,' he said. 'She told me that when William and her play Scrabble they don't usually finish it because one of them slams it shut.'

At a St Patrick's Day parade, where Kate presented traditional sprigs of shamrock to the officers and guardsmen of the 1st Battalion Irish Guards in Aldershot, she once more insisted that she did not know the sex of her child and disclosed that she and William were at odds over their personal choice.

When a guardsman asked her if she knew whether her unborn baby was a girl or a boy, she replied: 'Not yet,' and added, 'I'd like to have a boy and William would like a girl.'

The presentation of shamrocks by a senior female member of the

TOP: An engagement portrait of the royal couple made from jelly beans, March 2011.

BOTTOM: Paul Emsley with his controversial portrait of Catherine, which she described as 'brilliant'.

TOP: Catherine almost
comes a cropper when she
catches her heel in a grating
while presenting the Irish
Guards with shamrocks at
Aldershot on St Patrick's
Day, March 2013.

BELOW: Catherine
launches the *Royal Princess*
cruise liner at its berth in
Southampton.

royal family was started by Queen Alexandra, the wife of Edward
VII, in 1901. William, who wore ceremonial dress and was attending
the parade as colonel of the regiment, smiled as he too received a
sprig of shamrock from Kate. But there was a worrying moment
when she got the heel of her shoe caught in a drain cover and nearly
took a tumble before managing to grab hold of William's arm to
steady herself.

More used to being transported by chauffeur-driven limousine
these days, Kate travelled on a tube train to mark the 150th
anniversary of the London Underground system in March. While
touring the historic Baker Street station she was jokingly handed
a badge that some pregnant women wear on the tube system
bearing the slogan, 'baby on board.' The idea is to encourage other
passengers to offer them their seat if they are standing.

Chief operating officer, Howard Collins told her, 'They're fantastic,
they really do make a difference. It saves men the embarrassment of having
to guess if a woman is pregnant.'

Kate, who was taken on the tour with the Queen and Prince Philip,
got a laugh when she replied, 'I'll wear this at home!' She later told Mr
Collins that she used to be a regular traveller on the underground and that
she missed it.

Launching the cruise ship was *Royal Princess*, in Southampton on 14
June, Catherine's last engagement before taking 'maternity leave' from
her royal duties. Although no actual due date had been given for the new
arrival, it was expected in July and speculation was rife about precisely
when the baby would be born and what it would be called. All that was
known for sure was that the baby would be titled HRH and would be
Prince or Princess of Cambridge.

Bookmakers Ladbrokes took bets on almost 100 different names, with
traditional Royal Family names Alexandra for a girl and George for a boy
as favourites. What no one knew was whether the baby was to be a boy or
a girl. On a visit to Cumbria with the Princess Royal as late as 17 July, the
Queen was asked by a little girl whether she was hoping for a boy or a girl
and Her Majesty replied, 'I don't think I mind but I would very much like
it to arrive because I'm going on holiday soon!'

In a summer of sport reflecting the previous year's British Olympic
triumphs in London, the British and Irish Lions enjoyed a historic test
series victory over Australia and the following day, on 7 July, Andy Murray
became the first Men's Singles Champion at Wimbledon for 77 years. On
any other year, Catherine would have been delighted to sit in the Royal

Box on Centre Court to watch Murray's victory, but with temperatures hitting 40° Celsius on court, the heavily pregnant duchess would have been extremely uncomfortable, to say the least.

Mid-July was the closest most came to predicting the day the baby would arrive but the press took up station outside St Mary's Hospital in Paddington, London, from the beginning of the month, the pavement opposite the hospital cluttered with an ever-increasing forest of ladders on which photographers would stand to try to get that all-important first photo of the royal baby.

On 22 July, Catherine arrived at St Mary's and at 4.24 pm the baby was born. Following tradition a messenger delivered a note to the Queen confirming the sex of the baby and a notice was then posted outside Buckingham Palace, with Clarence House setting a modern trend by posting a message on Twitter. It was a boy.

Born weighing 8lb 6oz, his full name was announced on 24 July as George Alexander Louis, to be known as His Royal Highness Prince George of Cambridge, the third in line to the throne.

RIGHT: The first appearance of Catherine and her baby son, on the steps of the Lindo Wing.

BOTTOM: The world's press wait for news of the birth, outside St Mary's Hospital in Paddington.

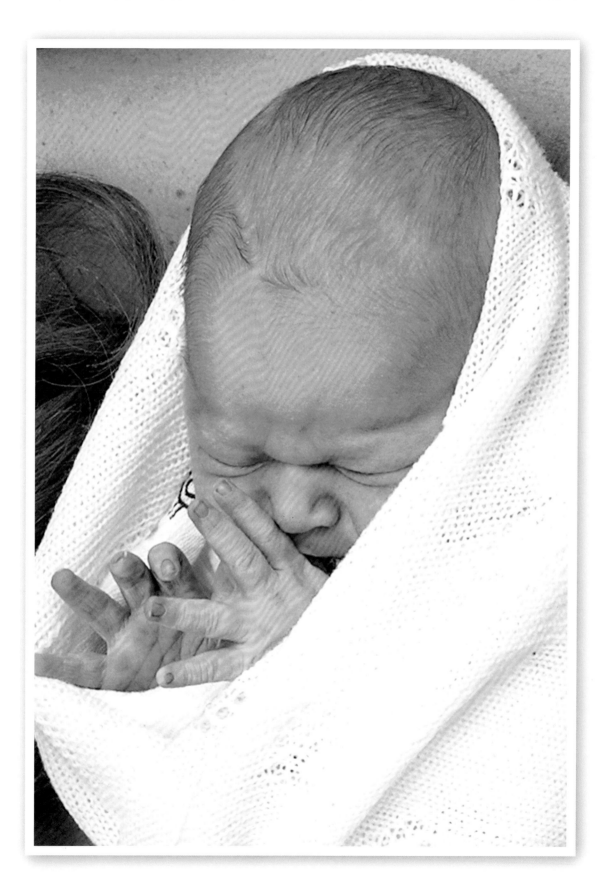